GW01032655

Hydropo

A Beginner's Guide to Building an Ideal Hydroponic Garden for Growing Vegetables, Herbs and Fruits

By

Alfred McJames

© **Copyright 2020 by (Alfred McJames) - All Rights Reserved**

This document is geared towards providing exact and reliable information in regard to the topic and issue covered. The publication is sold with the idea that the publisher is not required to render accounting, officially permitted, or otherwise, qualified services. If advice is necessary, legal or professional, a practiced individual in the profession should be ordered.

- From a Declaration of Principles which was accepted and approved equally by a Committee of the American Bar Association and a Committee of Publishers and Associations.

It is not legal in any way to reproduce, duplicate, or transmit any part of this document in either electronic means or in printed format. Recording of this publication is strictly prohibited and any storage of this document is not allowed unless with written permission from the publisher. All rights reserved.

The information provided herein is stated to be truthful and consistent, in that any liability, in terms of inattention or otherwise, by any usage or abuse of any policies, processes, or directions contained within is the solitary and utter responsibility of the recipient reader. Under no circumstances will any legal responsibility or blame be held against the publisher for any reparation, damages, or monetary loss due to the information herein, either directly or indirectly.

Respective authors own all copyrights not held by the publisher.

The information herein is offered for informational purposes solely and is universal as so. The presentation of the information is without contract or any type of guarantee assurance.

The trademarks that are used are without any consent, and the publication of the trademark is without permission or backing by the trademark owner. All trademarks and brands within this book are for clarifying purposes only and are the owned by the owners themselves, not affiliated with this document.

Table of Contents

Introduction

Hydroponics is part of hydroculture and is an effective approach used to grow plants using the water-based nutrient solution without the need for soil use. Some materials such as perlite, gravel, pea stone, and many others are used instead of dirt as a growing medium, which provide excellent assistance for the root system and the plant. Nutrients are transported to the roots of plants with the help of water. In soil plants, roots have to be grown for nutrients, while roots do not have to look for food in the hydroponic system. This system allows plants to grow in small or large containers, without even having a real soil garden. In general, all hydroponic systems have a tank in which water and nutrients are stored, and a garden bed is mounted. Water circulates in the plants providing, and in this system, no electricity or appliances are involved.

Growing with hydroponics has many benefits, the greatest of which is a much higher growth rate in your plants. Your plants will mature up to 25 percent faster with the proper setup and produce almost 30 percent than the same plants grown in soil. Your plants grow more quickly because they do not have to work to get nutrients so hard. Even a small root system can supply the plant with the exact amount it needs so that it focuses more on upstream growth than downstream root expansion. All of this is achievable by carefully monitoring the nutrient solution and the pH values. As the system is enclosed, a hydroponic system may use less water than soil-based plants, which leads to less evaporation. Whether you believe it or not, hydroponics is healthier for the environment because of the reduction of soil waste and pollution.

The great thing about hydroponics is that multiple types of hydroponic systems are available.

You can choose the one which fits the most. Some of the best systems in the hydroponic industry incorporate multiple hydroponics into one integrated hydroponic system. Hydroponics is different in that there are many methods that you can use to get your plants to the nutrient solution.

With the use of the hydroponic system, you can grow just about anything for seasoning or medicinal purposes, along with most house plants, flowering plants, vegetables, many sorts of fruit, and an infinite variety of herbs. The indoor gardening under growing lights gives you unparalleled flexibility at any time of year to grow almost anything. Fresh fruit, vegetables, and herbs may be supplied throughout the year by hydroponic gardening. You can also flourish your own flowers or leaves and decorate your home regardless of season or weather. The choices depend upon individual preferences and are nearly endless.

Deploying your very own hydroponic DIY garden tends to come with a whole network of advantages. It does not matter how ample or minor your space is; you can design your garden and see it flourish. These often use far less water than conventional gardens and are less susceptible to harmful pesticides. As these types of gardens preserve water and do not diminish the soil, they are friendly to the environment. Moreover, they yield the same flavorful crops you'd find in conventional gardens.

For all kinds of growers, hydroponics is an ideal choice. It is an excellent option because it helps you to carefully monitor the factors that influence your plants' growth. A perfectly designed hydroponic system can maintain plant quality and the quantity of produced yield. If you want to grow the largest, most succulent, and leafy plants, hydroponics is the right option for you.

At first, it may seem annoying with all the machinery and work involved, but once you get the hold of the basics, it will all seem easy enough. Start small, keep that simple and your hydroponic system will never stop surprising you.

Chapter 1: Introduction to Hydroponics

Hydroponics is the soilless method of growing plants. You may have heard of "soil-less culture," which is a common name for saying the same thing if you have not heard of hydroponics. The same natural conditions needed to grow plants in soils are used, with the benefit that weeds or soil-borne pests and diseases do not affect the plants. Hydroponic systems have been in use for centuries, although they may seem to be a new technology. The hydroponics used in earliest years was Babylon's hanging garden, Kashmir's floating garden, and the Aztecs of Mexico, who used rafts for plants on shallow lakes. Also, hieroglyphic records from several hundred years B.C. in Egypt. Describe the cultivation of water-based plants. More recently, in the South Pacific during the Second World War, mobile hydroponic farms were used to feed troops.

Hydroponics is now beginning to play an even more significant role in agricultural production worldwide. Rising demographics, climatic shifts, water shortages in some areas and poor-quality water are all factors that influence the movement towards alternative horticulture methods. Hydroponics helps many to get fresh foods where they would usually require it to be brought in or kept for long periods. A prime example of this is the naval submarines, where hydroponics is used to provide fresh fruit and vegetables to the crew hydroponics are more useful in developing countries, where intensive processing of food in limited areas is provided. Hydroponics enables you to grow plants more effectively, using up to 95 percent less water than ground-based horticulture in some cases. Hydroponics can give you a better-quality plant at a higher yield. The only limitations to a successful hydroponic system are water and nutrient availability. The desalinated seawater can be used in places where freshwater is not available.

1.1 What is Hydroponics?

The term hydroponics derives from two Greek words, "hydro," which means water and "ponics," which means work. By definition, hydroponics is a process of growing plants in a water-based nutrient-rich solution. Hydroponics uses no soil. Instead of using water, it protects the root system using an inactive material such as perlite, rock wool, clay pellets, peat moss, or vermiculite. The basic principle regarding hydroponics is to enable the plant roots to come into direct contact with the solution of nutrients, while also gaining access to oxygen, which is necessary for proper growth. The term hydroponics derives from the Greek language. Its meaning is "working with water" and is a process of growing plants in liquid enriched in nutrients rather than soil.

Hydroponics can be done indoors during the warm weather and outdoors throughout the year, including the following advantages:

- no weeding
- rapid growth
- high yields in a small space
- no requirements
- stealing crops
- clean vegetables
- easy to harvest
- no soil-related insects or diseases

One of the main things about hydroponics is that it can be done in a small space — in a balcony or terrace, a small yard, a rooftop.

Since it is a self-contained method, it is easy to scale a hydroponics setup to any size you wish (keeping in mind the water) to do something for yourself, a companion, or your relatives.

pH Stability in Hydroponic Systems

Control of the pH of the hydroponic garden is essential in hydroponics. If pH is suitable for every plant, nutrients are absorbed and optimally developed. A pH control of the solutions of nutrients involves the use of non-precise, liquid test sets, or even better pH meters of paper strips. Every plant has its own pH requirements, and you can control them easily by adding a pH-adjuster solution to the nutrient water to reach the desired level. In any hydroponic supply store, you can find the pH-adjuster solution. Phosphoric acid is the most common approach to lower pH, and potassium hydroxide is used to raise pH. The pH of the solution raises as the plant uses the nutrient. The pH must be monitored and adjusted periodically if required.

Nutrients in Hydroponics

The system adds hydroponic fertilizers to the water to help the vegetables grow. There are two types of fertilizer: Powder and Liquid. The best use for beginner gardeners and small systems is liquid fertilizers, which consist of a mixture of various ratios of concentrated nitrogen, phosphorus, and potassium. Powdered fertilizers are used in large hydroponic systems and are more complex to use than liquid ones. You can choose the mixture of nutrients best suited to your hydroponic garden.

1.2 History of Hydroponics

Across history, several different civilizations have used hydroponic growing techniques. As noted in Howard M. Resh's Hydroponic Food Production, "Babylon's hanging gardens, the floating gardens of the Mexican Aztecs, and those of the Chinese are examples of' Hydroponic' culture" (5th ed. Woodbridge Press, 1997, p. 23). Egyptian hieroglyphic records from hundreds of B.C. describe plant growth in water. So, hydroponics is hardly a new cultivation method. In this creative area of agriculture, however, enormous progress has been made over the years. Scientists and horticulturists have experimented with various hydroponic methods throughout the last century. Hydroponics can be used as one of the potential applications of research in non-Arable areas around the world for growing fresh. It is a matter of the fact that some people in their area are unable to grow in the soil if there is even soil. This hydroponic application took place during World War 2. Troops were supplied with fresh products grown in established hydroponic systems stationed at non-arable islands of the Pacific.

Hydroponics was incorporated in the space program, later in the century. Hydroponics fit easily into their sustainability plans as NASA presumed the practicalities of detecting a society on another planet or the Earth's moon. This research is still ongoing. But there were not only scientists and analysts who were involved in Hydroponics by the 1970s. Traditional farmers and enthusiastic hobbyists started to get the advantages of hydroponic production. Some of the hydroponics' positive aspects include:

- The potential to produce higher yields than conventional soil-based agriculture.
- Allows food in parts of the world that cannot sustain soil crops to be grown and processed.

- Eliminates the need for massive use of pesticides (considering that most pests live in the soil), efficiently clean up our air, water, soil, and food.

Commercial growers flock like never before to the Hydroponics. The ideals of these strategies impact issues that are important to most people, including helping to end poverty in the world and making things cleaner. People worldwide have built their own systems to grow delicious, fresh food for their families and friends. Educators realize how wonderful Hydroponics can be in the classroom. Ambitious people are working to make their dreams come true by living in their greenhouse backyard, selling their yield to local markets and restaurants.

As now, many people are involved in hydroponics and related disciplines, such as aeroponics, aeroponics, and aquaponics, so its progress has become faster than ever.

Timeline of Modern Hydroponic Development

Scientific experiments on plant growth & constituents were not recorded until 1600. In his experiment, the Belgian Jan Van Helmont indicated that plants were obtaining substances from water. He did not know, however, that plants also need airborne carbon dioxide and oxygen. In 1699 John Woodward went on to study plant growth using water culture. He found plants grow best in water, which contained the most soil. So, he concluded that these were certain compounds in the soil-derived water which led to the growth of the plant, rather than the water itself. A number of subsequent studies were carried out until 1804 when De Saussure proposed that plants get comprised of chemical components absorbed from water, soil, and air.

The French chemist Boussignault went on to verify this proposal in 1851. He experimented with cultivating plants without soil in an insoluble unnatural media, which includes sand, quartz, and charcoal. He used only nutrients, such as water, media, and chemical. The dry matter of plants contains hydrogen and carbon as much as the oxygen that comes down from the air; plants consist of nitrogen and other mineral nutrients. He also finds that plants need water and obtains hydrogen from it. The 1860 and 1861 marks the end of an extensive search for the essential nutrient source for plant growth when the first standard formula for the nutrient solutions, dissolved in water, was provided to the plants by two German botanists, Julius von Sachs, and Wilhelm Knop. This is where "nutriculture" originated. It is now called Water Culture. Through this method, plant roots were completely immersed in a water solution containing phosphorus (P), nitrogen (N), potassium (K), magnesium (Mg), sulfur (S), and calcium (Ca). They now look like macro elements or macronutrients, which are relatively large-scale elements. Surprisingly, however, only experiments were conducted on the method of plants growing in water and nutrient solutions and used simply in plant research laboratories. The interest in applying the nutrition practice was noticed only when the greenhouse industry emerged in 1925. Researchers looked at issues with soil structure, fertility, and pests regarding soil cultural methods. They were dedicated to the advantage of nutrition for the production of large crops.

W.F. Gericke from the University of California at Berkeley has been experimenting with nutriculture for agricultural crop production in the early thirties. Initially, the term aquaculture was called but dropped after learning that it was used to describe the culture of aquatic organisms. In 1937, Setchell had recommended Gericke the term "hydroponics." Gericke started to publicize the practice of growing plants in a water solution while at U.C. Berkley. However, he encountered public and university skepticism. The use of on-site greenhouses in his study was declined even by his colleagues. Gericke said they were completely wrong when 25-meter high tomato plants were successfully grown in nutrient-filled solutions.

The university still questioned his positive cultivation account and asked two other students to examine his claim. The two carried out the research and reported their findings in the 1938 agricultural bulletin. They verified Hydroponics' application but concluded their research that crops grown with hydroponics are no healthier than those grown on quality soils. In comparison with cultural practice, however, they skipped many benefits of agricultural hydroponics. The benefits every hydroponic grower nowadays knows by heart.

The earliest well-known use of Hydroponic plant cultivation was on Wake Island, a soilless island in the Pacific Ocean, in the early 1940s. Pan American Airlines used this island as a refueling stop. The lack of soil has meant that growing with the cultural method is impossible, and the airlifting of fresh vegetables was incredibly expensive. Hydroponics solved the problems excitingly well and supplied the entire troops on this distant island with fresh vegetables. Hydroponic cultivation remained widespread in the military after World War II. The U.S. military planted a 22 ha at Chofu, Japan. In the 1950s, Hydroponics' soilless method expanded to a range of countries, including England, France, Italy, Spain, Sweden, the USSR, and Israel.

Present Hydroponic Application

With Hydroponics distinct advantages such as higher growth rate, space saver, water efficiency, and better pest and disease control, it is no wonder that hydroponics has been widely applied around the world. For every greenhouse grower, it has become an essential part. Nearly all greenhouse farms use certain types of hydroponics to produce their trees and food.

As per the International Greenhouse Vegetable Production-Statistics (2017 Edition), the total commercial greenhouse vegetable production area was estimated at 489,214 hectares. It reports that most countries in the world have built greenhouses, and the largest of them is in the developing countries, namely the United States, Canada, the Netherlands, and Australia. They must provide 2 million pounds per year of fresh leafy lettuce.

Future of Hydroponics

We find thousands of inventions and improvements in the history of hydroponics. At first, the hydroponics was slow, throughout history. We are in an age of rapid growth as with any other technological progress. As we have seen with aerospace research, hydroponic systems can be supposed to precede any space colonization.

New and more accessible hydroponic methods will surely come into play. Due to the high efficiency and environmental advantages of hydroponics, problems in traditional soil farming have already been examined. It is not a far-reaching leap to assume hydroponic overtaking farming in the agriculture sector. Regardless, we can look at history and the fact that hydroponics was a crucial element in human development. That will always continue, just as human nature's drive to improve, innovate, and find creative ways to bring prosperity to our societies will continue.

1.3 Essential Components of Hydroponics

Hydroponic systems vary, but they have similar significant components as well. These comprise what the system needs to be perfect and function as necessary to avoid failures.

You can choose to work with the kits already available in the market, or you may choose to build one as an individual.

Whatever you choose, there are some important components everybody will need. This will include growing media, grow light supplies, and a nutrient solution. You will also need to envision the routine maintenance.

Grow Light Supplies

The cultivation of indoor plants requires lighting, which closely resembles that of the sun. You need to have a full spectrum of light in this. There are various types of light solutions in this based on the plants you wish to grow. Fluorescent lights are perfect for foliage plant growth as they add natural light despite the lack of a full spectrum.

On the other hand, it will require better lighting for flowering plants and vegetables and, thus, the use of metal halide lights. These are intended for closest sunlight similarities. High-pressure sodium lights are also important, and it should be noted that they offer a more excellent range of red/orange spectrum. These are essential for the photosynthesis process and the production of chlorophyll. To help boost the lighting efficiency, you may include light movers or reflectors.

Do not overdo it to prevent plant burning and death.

Growing Medium

What replaces the soil in natural cultivation is a growing medium. There are various growing mediums, and based on the type of hydroponics, you can choose the finest medium to work with. Growing mediums keep all the nutrients you would need to grow.

Rockwool and expanded clay are the most popular mediums used, as they offer more advantages compared to other mediums. It is not, however, limited to just these two, and others may use sand, gravel, bark, coconut fiber, vermiculite, polyurethane foam, and perlite as well.

- Rockwool has the added benefit of keeping more water content while simultaneously boosting the circulation of air with the roots.

- The expanded clay has the added benefit of fostering air circulation. It is also pH neutral, and over time, so it won't be compacted to make it durable.

Nutrient Solution

It is the nutrient solution that holds all the nutrients that your plants need. The solution is water and the nutrients that are contained in a reservoir. Water with minimum residue should be soluble in the solution. Even better, it is advisable to have a solution without residues, as this will not minimize maintenance needs. Make sure you change the solution as required for 1 to 2 weeks.

It is recommended to go for a hydroponic nutrient solution, as it has the required ratios of the nutrients needed. It also avoids a level of toxicity to your plants. It is best to test the electrical conductivity level before you can settle for a nutrient solution. The conductivity gauge is used to do this. Note that a high electrical conductivity in comparison to flowers and fruit entails a vegetative growth. The amount will vary considering other factors like plant quantity, and plant age as younger plants will consume less. Additional factors will be based on the hydroponics type.

Nutrient Reservoir

The solution is then placed to be used here before the plants have access to the solution. It is not restricted to what you could use as a reservoir of nutrients. A large plastic container or any device, that can hold as much water as you need, can be used.

While you may choose from different materials, however, it is best to avoid reservoirs made of metallic materials. This is because other components are likely to be introduced, which are deemed harmful to the plants. Strong plastic is recommended because it is also easier to clean and maintain even a novice in hydroponics for anyone.

Grow Tray

A grow tray is used to hold the plants. Many believe the plants are placed in the solution of nutrients, but this is not the case. Plants are segregated from each other. The plants are grown in the growing tray, or what is commonly called a grow chamber. Others especially use pots for small-scale cultivation. That will also vary depending on the hydroponics' type. A supplier will lead you through the advantages and difficulties of using one grow tray versus another.

Pump

A pump is used to pump water out of the reservoir. Its main function is to oxygenate the water and keep the reservoir from growing algae. This is similar to an aquarium. The circulation facilitates ensuring the water is clean and fresh. Each hydroponic system must have a pump in it. Make sure it does not block, as this will affect the plants negatively. Monitor its functionality constantly to avoid any blockages.

Air Stone

An air stone is usually included, although this is not a fundamental necessity. It is strongly recommended since it serves to add oxygen to the nutrient solution. Even for conventional cultivation, oxygen is required to enhance germination and healthy growth overall. More production of oxygen means you will boost faster growth and keep the nutrient solution fresh for use.

1.4 Significance of Hydroponics

Everyone knows that plants need minerals and water for growth. During this process, carbon dioxide is required to absorb from the atmosphere. Plants require photosynthesis basically, but it does perform metabolic functions as well as transpiration and absorption. Soil is a core medium of the plant that absorbs nutrients from the water. The soil is only a medium, and the basic need for the plant is minerals. This is the principle of hydroponics. The speed of plant growth is the main primacy for hydroponics over soil cultivation. When you are growing anything in the soil or watering your crop, you feed the soil and not the crop. Then the soil holds the nutrients and makes them available to the plant. Hydroponics is of great significance. There are several advantages of hydroponics which are as follow:

Advantages of Hydroponics

No Soil Required

In some cases, you can plant crops in areas that do not produce crops or are heavily contaminated. Hydroponics was widely used in the 1940s to provide fresh vegetables for soldiers in Wake Island, a Pan American airline refueling station. This is the Pacific Ocean's distant arable region hydroponics has also been regarded by NASA as the potential farming to grow food for astronauts in space (where there is no soil).

Better Use of Space and Location

Since every plant is supplied and maintained in a system, you can expand in your small apartment as long as you have other areas, or in the spare bedrooms.

The roots of plants typically grow and spread in search of food, and in soil, oxygen.

Hydroponics does not do this because the roots are submerged in a tank full of oxygenated solutions and interact directly with essential Minerals. You can, therefore, grow your plants a lot closer while saving massive amounts of space.

Climate Control

Hydroponic growers can have complete control over the climate temperature, light intensification, and air composition as in greenhouses. In that way, whatever the season is, you can grow food all year round. Farmers should produce food at the right time to maximize profits for their businesses.

Hydroponics Water Saving

Hydroponically grown plants use just 10 percent of the water compared to those cultivated on the ground. Water is recirculated as in this method, plants will take the water they need while the run-off ones will be caught and added to the system. Water loss happens only in two ways-evaporation and device leaks (but a successful hydroponic setup will reduce or have no leakage). Agriculture is expected to use up to 80 percent of land and surface water in the United States. Water will become a key issue in the future because the FAQ estimates that food production would rise by 70 percent. Hydroponics is considered a legitimate option for large-scale food production.

Effective Use of Nutrients

In hydroponics, you have 100 percent control over the nutrients required by plants. Until planting, growers should test what plants require and how much nutrients they need at different levels and combine them with water appropriately. Nutrients are preserved in the tank, so there are no nutrient shortages or changes like they are in the soil.

pH Control of the Solution

The minerals in the water are stored. It ensures that the pH of your water mixture relative to the soils is much easier to measure and modify. It ensures optimal plant absorption of nutrients.

Better Growth Rate

You are your own boss who controls the entire environment for the growth of your plant's temperature, lights, humidity, and particularly nutrients. Plants are positioned in ideal conditions, while nutrients are supplied in sufficient quantities, and the root systems come into direct contact. Plants are no longer wasteful of valuable resources looking for diluted soil nutrients. Instead, they turn their entire focus on raising and producing fruit.

No Weeds

You will understand how annoying weeds affect your garden once you have worked in the soil. To gardeners, it is one of the most time-consuming jobs as it involves plow and hoe. Weeds are mostly soil related. So, clear the soils, and all weed structures are gone. Hydroponics eases much of your difficulty because it says goodbye to weeds.

Fewer Diseases and Pests

Like weeds, getting rids of soil helps to make your plants less prone to soil-borne pests such as birds, gophers, groundhogs, and diseases such as the species Fusarium, Pythium, and Rhizoctonia. Also, when growing indoors in a closed system, gardeners can easily take care of most environmental variables.

Less Use of Insecticide and Herbicides

Since you don't use soils, and while weeds, pests, and plant diseases are greatly reduced, fewer chemicals are used.

It really helps you grow healthier and cleaner foods. Insecticide and herbicide cutting is a strong point of hydroponics when the standards for modern life and food safety are gradually being placed on top.

Labor and Time Savor

In addition to investing less on the tilling, watering cultivation, and fumigation of weeds and pesticides, you can save lots of time. More, the growth of plants is shown to be higher in the hydroponic fields, which saves time. Hydroponics has potential in it when agriculture is expected to be technologically focused.

Stress-relieving Hobby

The passion will bring you back into touch with nature. Tired after a long day of work and traveling, you are back to your small corner of the apartment; it is time to lay it all back and play with your hydroponic garden. Reasons such as lack of spaces no longer make sense. In your little closets, you can grow fresh, tasty vegetables, or essential herbs, and enjoy a pleasant time with your little green spaces.

Chapter 2: Types of Hydroponic Systems

Hydroponics is a popular plant growing method that uses a nutrient-rich water-based solution, which means that soil is not used in a hydroponic system. Plant's roots are instead supported by materials such as peat, clay, perlite, and rock wool. There are thousands of variations of hydroponics systems available for you when you want to build or utilize a hydroponic system for growing plants.

At first, it may seem complicated how hydroponic systems work, but once you understand it, it is quite simple to see how they work. Hydroponic systems (Drip System, Ebb & Flow, N.F.T., Water Culture, Aeroponics, and Wick) are available in six types. All hydroponic systems simply rely upon these six different types, regardless of what they may call them, either one type or two or more of the six types. There are countless ways to change and alter any element of any of the six systems. So, once you know how each of the three roots of each hydroponic system needs water, nutrients, and oxygen; you will be able to identify the type of system in which hydroponics is.

All kinds of hydroponic systems work differently, so all six systems have their own distinct advantages and disadvantages to be considered. You should understand how each system works to get full insight into how to use the one you select when you are ready to use a hydroponic system for growing plants. The following offers a thorough and detailed examination of six kinds of hydroponic systems to help you determine the right system.

2.1 Nutrient Film Technique (N.F.T.)

Everyone dreams that their homes have a pretty green space. But what is more than a garden you can both use and enjoy? Of course, a suitable type of hydroponic! The nutrient film technique (or N.F.T. system) system is popular in the field of soilless farming for the simple also the effective design of hydroponic growers.

The technique of the nutrient film is often used for growing smaller and faster plants like various types of lettuce. In addition, this system is also used by commercial farmers to make grasses and strawberries. Nutrient Film Technique is versatile as well as a famous hydroponic system with different configurations and the same components as Ebb and Flow.

A nutrient film technique system can be designed in various ways; however, they all go down to the tubing after creating a very shallow nutrient solution. When they come into contact with water, the plants' bare roots take up the nutrients in the solutions.

For one reason, the N.F.T. system is similar to the Ebb as well as Flow technique: both use water pumps to supply your plants with nutrients. But the N.F.T. system continuously flows, unlike a flood & drain mechanical system for an Ebb and Flow setup.

Working of N.F.T.

1. A reservoir containing a nutrient solution.

2. Nutrient pump.

3. Tubes for the distribution of water to the N.F.T. growing tubes from the nutrient pump.

4. Channel to grow in the plants.

5. Net pots to contain seedlings and to grow crops.

6. Return system (tubing, channel) to redirect the used solution of nutrients back to the reservoir.

Two main components exist in the N.F.T. system: the grow tray (or channel) as well as the water and nutrient reservoir. In the grow tray, net pots are there, which contain the growing media for holding plants and nutrients in the nutrient solution (perlite, cocoa, Rockwool). However, most growers do not actually use an N.F.T. system for growing media, as the roots have enough moisture, nutrients, and oxygen. The plant roots become a dense mat in the channel, and the leaves are placed on the top, supported sometimes by a trellis system. N.F.T. is supplied with a pump to the grown tray and a drained water pipe to recycle the unoccupied water nutrient solution.

How do you do that? The grow tray is placed at the angle to let the water flow down towards the return tube. This tray is supported by a rack or a bench. The extra water nutrient solution will flow from this pipe and then recirculate again through the system into another channel or tube.

The roots of plants hang down to the ground where the shallow film of the nutrient solution comes into contact and absorbs nutrients. The nutrient solution's thin-film permits that the plants are watered but not completely soaked. The upper portion of the roots can also stay dry and gain access to oxygen in the air.

Tools of NFT

THE GROW TRAY is a major part of an N.F.T. system. It uses slightly downward pipes or channels rather than flat trays to allow all the nutrient solutions to go through their roots. It is also easy to set the growing tray at an angle with tubes or channels. The channels usually consist of a P.V.C. pipe, plastic film, or round tube. On the P.V.C. pipe, the net pots and seedlings are fitted with holes. If you are a hydroponic amateur, these materials are cheap and simple to obtain.

The use of P.V.C. as a material has one drawback; however, the film doesn't evenly cover the roots. The roots in the center have access to a deeper solution, while the roots closest to the borders only have access to a shallow depth. You need to use a flat channel to resolve this issue.

Seedlings are placed in two ways.

Option 1 is to directly place the seedlings in the P.V.C. pipeline or channel holes.

Option 2 is to place the seedlings in net pots and place them in the hole for greater stability.

The majority of farmers do not use N.F.T. systems for growing media. If you choose to use, make sure that you do not put much deep enough in the net pots for the roots to fall via the ground. Irrespective of the seedling method, the plant roots should often be checked and trimmed to prevent long roots, which might obstruct the system. The length of the growing tray is an important factor. The nutrient solution and oxygen levels decrease when the nutrient solutions flow across the roots. You can solve this problem by using "short-run" trays rather than long ones. "Short-run" trays ensure that plants receive nutrients of the same composition at the end of the line as those at the start of the line. By checking your pH and nutrient levels and refilling your solution, you can also eliminate this problem with "long-lasting" trays. It is time to switch to a short-run system if you notice plants at the end of the line that do not grow as high as the ones initially.

A high-end nutrient pump and the low-end nutrient return pipe connect the growing tray with the reservoir. The air pump is connected to an air stone externally inside the reservoir to oxygenate the water. The nutrient solution is contained by the reservoir because the N.F.T. system recirculates.

The size of the reservoir depends on your number of plants. You need a reservoir with a minimum capacity of 5 gallons if you wish to grow a system of 40-50 plants. You would add a gallon of capacity to grow each additional 20-25 salad plants. It is recommended that you have somewhat more volume rather than a short volume. Like other hydroponic systems, the N.F.T. system does not use an auto timer linked to the water pump, so the pump is constantly running. In case of power shortage, shortcomings, or system failures, this can cause a problem, make sure the pump is checked, the tube is regularly filled, and a backup is ready.

Pros and Cons

Pros

• Easy root examination to diagnose symptoms of the disease, adequacy of feed, etc.

• Low intake of water and nutrients.

• Friendly to the environment–minimize the risk of localized groundwater contamination.

• Contrary to media-based systems, issues such as supply, disposal, and cost can be avoided.

Similar to other machine styles, it is relatively easy to clean roots and components.

• pH and conductivity of the plant roots can be maintained by means of regular feed (and corresponding flushing), preventing localized salt growth.

Cons

• The roots dry out and get stressed very quickly if the stream of nutrient solution stops.

• The channels can warm up faster than the root region in a freshly planted system when exposed to the sun's intense light. Nevertheless, there is a cooling effect of the continuous stream of nutrient solution.

• The roots of vigorous plants can block the channels.

• Pump failure, especially in hot weather, can lead to plants' death in a few hours.

• Not acceptable for growing plants such as carrots, i.e., with large tap root systems.

• The saline water may not be the best choice in the N.F.T., compared to run-to-waste structures, as recirculating water salinity decreases gradually.

The N.F.T. system is a system that is very easy to set up and to operate. It's ideal for producing fast-growing plants in a few weeks. You can grow several leaves, lettuces of Bibb and Cos type, mustard greens, kale, several Oriental vegetables, and herbs with this system. The N.F.T. method can also be used to grow certain edible flowers like nasturtium and cakes, which may be used to supplement salads & food presentations. This system can be used for fast results and seedlings for future harvests. This will satisfy every hobbyist's dream with a green area and a constant supply of goods.

2.2 Deep Water Culture (DWC)

Deepwater culture hydroponics is a system of hydroponic plant growth, with the roots suspended throughout the growing cycle in a nutrient solution. The center of the lid hangs in a net pot or cup, and the roots of the nutrient solution are suspended in a reservoir under the deck, which contains the solution of the nutrient.

An air pump and air supply device like an air stone is used to pump air into the reservoir. This keeps the amount of water supplied to the roots of the plant with oxygen. The pot or net cup is stuffed with a growing medium such as gravel, clay pellets, lava rocks, etc. The key to rapid growth is to ensure that the roots at least touch the water when the plants are young. As the plant grows and signs of the roots growing into the water, the water level can now drop.

Aeration of a hydroponic deep-water culture system is one of the system's most essential aspects. Let be explained; you would traditionally use an air pier to supply air to both the pot and reservoir. Ensure that air flows evenly across the whole reservoir or pot rather than providing greater air in a part of the reservoir or pot. You have a gap in the system when you see a void of air bubbling up at the top in your reservoir or pot. The following roots do not receive adequate air. The use of Air Injection Technology can remove this void. The air supply in the pot or reservoir is even. Nothing can hide its roots, and anywhere in the pot or reservoir, they can be revealed to air and oxygen. For example, you have a void of about 7 inches if you are cultivated in a bucket of 5 gallons and used a 3-inch air stone. This is an empty area; now you've got roots revealed to the void zone, and they do not get the oxygen they need. It also tends to push roots into the void area by using an air-supplying system that does not equally distribute air to the whole reservoir or pot.

Critical Parts:

This solution has three critical parts:

Oxygen: Although the roots are submerged in water rather than soil (which has holes and gaps where air lives), water must be well oxygenated to prevent the plant from drowning. The air pump and the air stone are used for this.

Water: Think about this system as if you cultivate in soil and water your plants permanently, which is one of the reasons why you can grow hydroponic, you must never water again.

Nutrients: A good soil contains all the nutrients which a plant needs to thrive and flourish.

Since we do not have soil, we need to add nutrients to the oxygen-rich water to our plants.

For two reasons, this method is known as Deep Water Culture. One of them is usually a reservoir that holds a decent quantity of water. More water will make your nutrient solution more stable, which implies less supervision and upkeep for you.

The second reason is that you are immersed in water as much of the root mass. Other methods expose the root zone of your plant to air and imbibe it only a few hours a day (Ebb, as well as flow systems, are a great example of this). Most of the root system of your plant is immersed 24/7 in deep water culture.

Recirculating Deep Water Culture

The traditional method is wonderful for beginners, so what if you really want to reach the next level in your system? Most people move to an RDWC or a Recirculating Deep-Water culture system when you want to upgrade your garden. The very last thing you have to do is to have ten buckets; all of them require their own calibration as well as adjustment. Does it not make sense to have one primary reservoir as well as feed that nutrient solution in all ten buckets if you are cultivating the same plant in 10 different buckets?

You just invented the system of the RDWC if you said yes!

An example is here: You should love torturing yourself, in order to want to calibrate each bucket individually! If you have various buckets chained together, you might wonder how oxygenation occurs.

Just like having different nutrient solutions for each bucket is ineffective, running an air stone system for each bucket is ineffective. Here comes into play the recirculating section of the name. Water shuts around through the spray pours, which oxygenate the water when it moves from bucket to bucket. This alteration to the classic DWC system is beautiful because only additional water from a central location must be calibrated, oxygenated, and immediately fed to all buckets.

The best analogy is the power grid; in our homes, we do not operate our own generators. The electricity is generated from central locations, and then sent into our homes via the power grid.

Bubbleponics

Although Bubbleponics is not seen by many and to be so different from traditional DWC, it has some benefits and is sufficiently important for discussion. Although Bubbleponics is a crazy name, the adaptation is simple. Bubbleponics wants to speed up this process by adding a nutrient solution to your plants for the first weeks rather than waiting until your plants get germinated, and the roots get on top of your reservoir. All that is working here is a water pump, with a drip line running from the tank to the net pots in which your plants sit. It is simple but highly efficient to accelerate germination and seedling in the life cycle of a plant.

Pros and Cons:

Pros:

For several different reasons, DWC systems are popular, primarily because they are one of the easiest types of systems, to begin with. A wicking system is the only system which is simpler.

Some other advantages are here for a DWC system to grow:

- Extremely low maintenance once it has been established.

- Extremely rapid growth as compared to soil. (I have cultivated lettuce in 30 days instead of 60 days in soil).

- Very small moving parts and mounting as well.

Cons:

But not all of this is sunshine and roses. Some troubles can cause problems with this type of system. However, they can mostly be avoided if you maintain your garden:

- pH, water, and nutrient concentration can fluctuate wildly in small systems.

- The ability to over or under calibrate is quite simple in small systems because of small dimensions.

- You may drown your roots into a low-oxygen nutrient solution in the case of an electron failure or a pump failure.

- The consistent temperature of the water can be difficult to maintain.

2.3 Wick Hydroponics

Wick method hydroponics is the easiest and simplest thing to do in both form and feature in the hydroponic world. As you see, these systems require only four components, and for those of you who love reuse and upcycling, you can easily develop a functioning system from everyday home items. Perhaps the trickiest part is to choose what to use for your wicks because there are too many materials. Hydroponics Wick system is the easiest of all six hydroponic systems. The name relates to the fact that those systems profit from wicking to feed the roots of plants with a water-based nutrient solution.

The four basic components of each hydroponic wick system are:

- The growing container
- Nutrient solution reservoir
- The growing medium
- Wicks

The growing container is situated a short distance over the reservoir, and wicks are positioned so that it extracts the nutrient-based solution from the reservoir and transfers them into the growing medium.

Working of Wick Hydroponics

Capillary action in a hydroponic wick system feeds the nutrient solution into the plant root area. Capillary action is the procedure used to extract liquid from a surface by sponges and paper towels. Once you came out of the park or outside patio chair and figured out that your back was wet, yes, you were a target of the capillary action of interacting with your clothing. It is also like a candle wick draws out wax or the oil lamp wick pulls up the fire where the fires go–so the word wicking is also used to explain the same process.

Wick hydroponics system is a passive hydroponics form that allows the system to work without motors, pumps, or moving components. Nevertheless, this does not allow you to use any type of machine. Instead, it simply describes the system's basic operation. Yes, these simplistic hydroponic systems often include a pump to pressurize the nutrients solution, but it is not essential for the system to work. The capillary action transfers the fluid itself to the roots.

Reason for Choosing Wick Hydroponics

One of the major reasons for picking hydroponics wick systems is that this hydroponic system is the friendliest to the environment. You do not need any electricity to grow plants in the places where your plants get plenty of natural light. For all your system components, you can select to use recycled as well as renewable materials. And water and nutrients consumed by hydroponic wick systems are lower than others. The other principal reason for choosing the hydroponic wick system is its elegant simplicity. For those who are just starting hydroponics, this makes an excellent starting project. The device can be built to be very basic and maintenance-free. Only the nutrient solution reservoir has to be replenished as required, and the machine must be flushed daily.

You don't have to use some specialized equipment with wick hydroponics. You can use a few buckets for your containers for a super simple system. Or, there is a nice way to make a 2-liter plastic bottle planting a mini wick scheme. Any material that is absorbent as for wicks can be used: strings, cords, yarns, or even cut old clothes strips.

Plants for which Wick Hydroponics are Best Suited

These are best suited for growing smaller plants, such as herbs and salad. It is also great for seeds and cuttings. The reason seems to be that wicking is a fairly slow and low-volume movement of liquid, and in comparison to other types, these plants don't need much.

Hydroponic wick systems are sometimes used to support higher plant growth in comparison to other growing systems. They are famous as salad and herb gardens in winter. And they could be used for plants to be grown elsewhere all year round.

Picking a Wick System Hydroponics Growing Container

This could vary from a standard bucket or plastic tub to a specially constructed grow tray. It contains the plants and the growing medium, which either can be placed together in separate individual containers or in a growing container. For the wicks to move in, you will have to make minor slits or holes on the surface of your container.

Keep in mind when planning this aspect of your method that you will need to flush out your growing medium on a regular basis so that you will make sure that it is ready for your growing container.

Advantages and Disadvantages of Wick System

Advantages

1. The main advantage of the Wick hydroponics system is that it is easy to build and easy to maintain. You may recycle or modify common household products and materials irrespective of whether you choose to keep them small or scale them up. You can enjoy low care gardening all year round when you have it up and running.

2. Another important benefit is that electricity is not required. For areas lacking access to electricity, and in countries that do not use electric power for artificial lighting, it becomes all the more efficient.

3. In terms of sustainability, water efficiency is very important to wick system hydroponics. The system is self-regulatory because the supply of the water-based solution itself is dependent on the plants' consumption of the solution.

4. However, because of the plant species it serves, hydroponic wick systems use fewer nutrients and water than that of other growing systems.

Disadvantages

1. The hydroponics of the wick system has a very significant drawback. The slow rate at which nutrient solution falls is quite constrained in which plants you are able to grow. Larger plants and fruit growers are more thirsted for the water and nutrients and are thus not well adapted for these cultivation schemes.

2. Another downside of the hydroponics wick system is that the growing medium will be prone to poisonous accumulation of nutrients over time. However, this problem could be easily avoided by rinsing it with fresh water every week or two.

2.4 Ebb and Flow- Flood and drain System

For many reasons, flood and drain systems (Ebb and Flow) are very popular with hydroponic growers. You can also use nearly every material you have located in to build them, as well as how easy it is for anyone, so you do not have to spend a lot of money on hydroponically grown plants. These can also be designed to suit any space available to you (indoors or outdoors). The various and creative methods of building them for that area are not constrained. Plants grow very well under flood and drain systems, as well as being cheap and easy to build. The flood and drain system basically works as it sounds just by flooding the nutrient solution in the plant root system. Perhaps continuously, nor regularly.

It is very simple to operate like a hydroponic flood & drain system. The main part of the flood & drain system includes the containers in which plants grow. It may be a single plant or a number of plants in series. A pump is switched on by a timer, and the water (Nutrient Solution) is pumped into the main section of the system using a submersible source/pond pump through tubing from the reservoir.

The nutrient solution fills the system until the height of the predetermined overflow tube is reached so that the roots of the plants are soaked. Around 2 inches underneath the top of the growing media is needed for an overflow tube.

If the flooding/filling system reaches the height of the overflow tube, it drains back into the reservoir, in which the system is recirculated. The overflow tube controls the water level of the flood and drain network and also guarantees that the pump does not spillover from the top of the system. Once the pump is stopped, the water drains back into the reservoir via the pump.

What do you need to create a Flood and Drain system (Ebb and Flow)?

- A reservoir in which the roots will grow.
- A nutrient solution container. (reservoir)
- A pump for the water fountain.
- A light timer is needed that will enable or disable the pump.
- Many tubing extends from the pump well into the reservoir to the flooding system.
- An overflow tube at the height of the water level is desired.
- Any kind of growing medium.

There are several options to create a flood and drain structure, so that small to medium-sized plants may expand very well. Even for the growth of large plants with greater flood and drain systems.

You can build one using the bucket, tubes, 2-liter bottles, storage containers, water bottle, old ice chest, trash cans, etc. It could be used for just about anything with water. The imagination is not stopped; the roots in the system can also be flooded and drained in many ways. Here are some examples of the three most common methods in which systems are flooded and drained.

(Tip 1) Try to ensure the air gets into the roof without water pouring out. A "T" connection can fit well with an extension a few inches above that of the waterline. It prohibits air pockets from developing and guarantees that they correctly flood and drain.

(Tip 2) Ensure that the overflow tube is larger than the inlet tube from the pump. If not, because the water just goes out through gravity and water comes in through the pump-action. You might wind upbringing in more water than the overflow is going out. This would cause the water to build up and spill out your system if you don't reduce the pump pressure (volume).

Types of Flood and Drain system setups

1. Plant Containers are Constructed in Sequence

This form of setup is most frequently used when watering (flooding) several separate containers of plants at the same time. It is necessary to keep in mind that with the Flood and Drain system, the plants are supposed to be watered above the reservoir like on bench or tabletop. Thus, by simple gravity, water may flow back to the reservoir, and thus drain the system properly.

First, various containers are all linked together by tubing, so that they all flood evenly and all at the same time when the structure is flooded. For convenience, there is typically just one overflow channel, instead of creating a separate overflow for each pipe being filled. This binds to the base system, to which all the containers are linked. And whenever the water level reaches the top point of the overflow, it pours over Ebb & Flow Flood and drain systems and returns to the reservoir to be pumped via the system again. The height of such an overflow tube will determine the height of the level of water in all associated containers (as long as it is stable) with the plants inside them. You may alter the height of the water in all the containers that are linked by simply changing the height of the sole overflow tube.

2. Flooding Tray Design

The flooding table/tray flood and drain (ebb and flow) setup are useful when you want to place plants in the system temporarily, have to move them around a lot, or Ebb & Flow Flood and drain table layout starting plants are to be placed in some other larger system. This technique floods only one container rather than flooding different containers with plants inside it. Generally, a container with a shallow rectangle or square shape sets on top of a table. The reservoir actually sits with easy access directly below.

Ebb & Flow Flood & drain table as flooded Water is drained from the reservoir into flooding tray on either side, and the overflowing on the other side flooding tray. This ensures that the water actually flows from one hand of the tray/table to another. Like any flood and drain system (Ebb and flow), the height of the overflow tube sets the height of the water during the flooding process and can also be adjusted as needed.

The plants are produced in standard plastic pots or containers and put as normal potted plants in the drain tray. Like traditional potted plants, though, the hydroponic growing medium is used instead of potting soil to pot the plants. Once the plants are sufficiently large, they can be transferred to a permanent hydroponic system.

One downside of using the flooding table is the growth of algae. That is why it should be regularly cleaned out. Since the top of the tray is generally left open, light in the lower part of the tray is allowed to enter the nutrient solution, which allows algae to grow. Alone the algae are not really harmful to the plants, but it uses dissolved oxygen in the atmosphere.

3. Surge Tank System

The flood and drain serge tank setup is helpful if a more vertical room is needed. Typically, the reservoir is always lower in flood and drain system than the hydroponic Ebb & Flow Flood as well as drain systems with a surge tank system. That's how water (nutrient solution) may drain out from the system by gravity back through overflow into the reservoir, and when the pump is off. But even when the level of water in the reservoir is greater than the hydroponic system, it is supposed to flood and drain back from; you could still set up a flood and drain system. That is when a surge tank is being used.

The flood and drain serge tank cost more to construct because many more parts are required. It operates on the central Ebb & Flow Flood & drain systems in the flooding process with a surge tank; the water is searching for its own level. In other terms, if they are paired underneath the waterline, the water height for one container would be the same in other containers. The surge tank acts as a temporary reservoir that regulates the height of water in all tanks having plants in them and is only complete during the process of floods.

The surge tank flood & drain (ebb and flow) system works by pumping water (nutrient solution) from the much greater main container into the surge tank when the pump time limit is going on. As the water level in the surge tank increases, at the same moment, the water level in all related plant reservoirs falls equally. Surge tank switches on a pump inside the surge tank when the level of water gets high enough. Then the pump inside the surge tank pumps water back to the main tank. Both the pumps are on at this time (pump in the main tank, and surge tank). The engine in the serge tank is already on after the timer for the device at the main reservoir turns off. The pump in the serge tank continues to pump all of the water back into the original reservoir (drain the system) until the level of water is low enough. At such a point, a 2nd float valve in the serge tank shuts off the pump.

2.5 Drip Hydroponics

Hydroponics' beauty depends on its flexibility. There is no proper way of creating a hydroponic system. You can choose any one-off at least half a dozen systems, depending on the space available, plant species, and other variables. Of these, a drip device is among the most popular & commercially viable solutions.

A drip system is an active hydroponic system. So, it uses a pump to supply the plants daily with water and nutrients. It is often classified as a trickle or micro-irrigation system. The system uses tiny emitters to stream the nutrient solution straight onto the plants. For hydroponics, a drip system is not special. Such a system is also extensively used for delivering nutrients and water to individual plants in outdoor gardens.

With both soil and growing media, it works extremely well. In reality, the drip system has been initially conceived in Israel for outdoor plant cultivation.

The system was designed to increase agricultural outdoor field production with water output. It was adapted successfully to the hydroponics later on. The emitters emit the liquid in a gradual soaking motion instead of blowing or running water at the plants. It means very less water is used in the structure. You have a higher degree of control over the quantity of water & nutrients; the plants are provided with. The system involves a network of feeder lines to supply the plants with water. This type of installation is better suited for huge growing operations. That is why commercial operations prefer drip hydroponics to other systems.

Working of Drip System

The system generally utilizes single plant pots. A network of pipes links the water from the reservoir to the plants. There have been two ways of exerting pressure on the water supply. It may be a normal water pump, or a system, based on gravity. Every single plant receives at least one committed drip emitter. Every emitter has processes that allow you to regulate the water flow. It contributes to the system's overall versatility; you can set differing flow rates for different plants.

In a drip system, the flow to the plants must be regulated. You need to give the growing media time to rest in between flows. A drip mechanism can overwhelm the plants if left unregulated, and ultimately kill them. Thus, all drip mechanisms use some sort of timer system to control water and nutrient flow to plants. The pump works many times a day in normal circumstances, to deliver water to the plants. Such a system necessitates significant initial preparation and commitment. But when the drip lines are mounted carefully, the machine will operate with minimal help. Such applications can be constructed to have a large level of automation.

Best Plants for Drip Irrigation System

A drip system is suitable for a wide range of herbs and plants, as it allows you better monitoring over the water & nutrient inputs. It also fits well with multiple growing media, so this further expands the system's reach.

Some of the plants you will cultivate using a hydroponic drip system are as follows:

- Lettuce
- Leeks
- Onions
- Melons
- Peas
- Tomatoes
- Radishes
- Cucumbers
- Strawberries
- Zucchini
- Pumpkins

The drip systems are known to be particularly suitable for larger plants. Such plants require wider growing media, which can hold greater amounts of moisture over a longer period of time. So, in a drip set up, the larger plants get suitable hydration and nutrition despite the slow watering system. A gradual draining medium is preferred for best results. Rockwool, peat moss or coconut coir are the most popular options in this group. Certain products such as clay pellets, perlite, and gravel may also be effectively used.

Pros & Cons of Drip system

A drip method has the following benefits:

- It allows greater control over delivering water and nutrients.

- Flexible, growth-scaling system.

- Low maintenance required, compared with other methods.

- Cheap and affordable deployment.

- Less possibility of system malfunction.

It also has the following disadvantages, particularly from a non-commercial viewpoint:

- It could be too complicated for a very minor grow operation.

- Maintenance is higher (for the reservoir) when using the water recycling method.

- If the non-recovery system is used, the possibility of waste arises.

2.6 Aeroponics

While the aeroponic system concept is rather basic, it is also the most technical of all six forms of hydroponic systems. Nonetheless, constructing your own simple aeroponic system is still fairly easy, and home many growers like growing in them too, and using this sort of hydroponic system even get very good results. Like any other form of hydroponic system, you can create it with many different types of materials, as well as with many different types of layout setups to fit into your room.

Some advantages of using an aeroponic system are typical that they use little or no growing media. The roots receive maximum nutrients, and as a result, the plants grow quicker. In general, aeroponic systems also use less water than any other kind of hydroponic system (particularly true aeroponic systems). Harvesting, particularly for root crops, is generally easier too.

There are, however, also some downsides of aeroponic systems, in addition, to be a bit pricier to construct. Through building up of the submerged mineral materials in the nutrient solution, the mister/sprinkler head can clog. And make sure that when they clog while you vacuum them, they have backups on hand to exchange. Even though the plant roots hang in mid-air by default in aeroponic structures, the plant roots are far more susceptible to drying out if the irrigation process stops. Thus, even temporary power outages (for whatever reason) may cause your plants to be dead much faster than any other sort of hydroponic system. In aeroponic structures, especially in the true high-pressure systems, there is also a decreased margin for error with the level of nutrients.

Types of Aeroponic Systems

1. Low-pressure Aeroponic (Soakaponic) Systems

Often named low-pressure aeroponic systems, "soakaponics" are what many people are known with when they talk of aeroponics. It is mainly because of the fact that most of the aeroponic devices sold in stores that offer hydroponics are low-pressure structures. Because the low-pressure systems operate very nicely, the size of the large water droplet varies greatly from that of the high-pressure systems.

The main reason why low-pressure aeroponic systems are so common is that they do not need much more expense or special equipment than other forms of hydroponic systems. The versatility & inexpensive low-pressure systems render this form of the aeroponic system particularly appealing to many home growers. While you do not need any special tools or a water pump, the regular pumps of the pool/pond will only do well. But, for any other form of hydroponic system, you want a pump that is better than you would. That is the main difference and the most important one.

That is because with every sprinkler head you attach, the pressure in the device should decrease more. The fountains, as well as pond pumps, do not give a psi (pressure) rating, however, the stronger the pump is the more GPH (gallons per hour) it might put out nearer to the "max head height."

You'll need enough sprinkler points to spread the water, to cover the whole root zone fully. Even though the plants get larger, and the density of the plant grows bigger. As the root mass grows big, penetration of the thick root mass is often difficult for the spray from sprinkler heads. If you build your low-pressure aeroponic system to spray the roots from above or near the top of the root mass, the water will trickle down via the root mass, much smarter than attempting to sprinkle them from below.

2. High-pressure Aeroponic Systems (True Aeroponic Systems)

While low-pressure systems are the most common, the "true aeroponic" systems are high-pressure aeroponics. This is because the higher pressure (60-90 psi) is required to effectively atomize the water into such a fine mist with a very limited droplet size of water. A fine mist enables a lot of oxygen to the roots than those in low-pressure structures. Creating a high-pressure aeroponic structure is, however, more complex and expensive.

What you will require to build your own true Aeroponic High-Pressure System:

- Accumulator Container (to behave as a Pressurized Tank).
- Solenoid valve. (to lock and unlock the Mister heads of the feed line)
- Cycle timer (a solenoid valve to be opened and closed).

- Fine mister heads. (to sprinkle the roots with such a fine mist)

- Tiny air compressor. (to give pressure the accumulator tank)

- Enclosed root zone growth area.

If you intend to recycle the nutrient solution, a collection reservoir for collecting the runoff is used; whereas the basic structure of the growing support chamber and plant can stay the same as with lower pressure systems. The delivery system for the water (nutrient solution) is very different. Because of the frequency with which a pump would need to switch on and off (100 to 1,000 times a day), this would serve out very quickly. For high-pressure aeroponic structures, the water pump is removed.

We pressurize the reservoir to do so. The simplest way to do that is to use an accumulator reservoir similar to ones used in RO water systems (reverse osmosis). It is essentially nothing but a tank in the middle with a rubber divider/diaphragm, which creates two sides. There is water (nutrient solutions) on one side, as well as compressed air on the other. The air is filled to about 60 to 90 psi until the pressure hits. That pressure forces against rubber diaphragm and squeezes the reservoir side to the same psi with a nutrient solution in it.

3. Ultrasonic Foggers

Ultrasonic foggers are most often used in aeroponic systems to produce mist but with mixed results. Ultrasonic foggers are widely used both on stage and in ponds to build optical displays. With Halloween decorations, they are often sold during Halloween too. Because they produce a mist with a really small water droplet size, very little real moisture is found in the mist/fog.

Often, the mist produced by ultrasonic foggers tends to fall to the bottom of the tank. Making it difficult to ensure the roots are all the time covered by the mist. Another problem with using foggers is that plates appear to clog with the buildup of minerals. The only plates which show some durability are the costly Teflon heads. These can be washed sometimes with white vinegar, or with water and pH down, and then wiped off with a Q-tip. In the same system, few growers merged the use of ultrasonic foggers with the aeroponic low-pressure layout.

2.7 Popular Variations of Hydroponic Systems

1. The Kratky Method

This approach is discovered by B.A. Kratky, from Hawaii University. Kratky can literally be regarded as Deep Water Culture, without a pump. While Deep Water Culture is an easy-to-build and simple technique among the six forms of hydroponic systems, it is easier and cheaper for Kratky. That's because farmers don't have to purchase the electronic devices with Kratky and don't need the electricity to run. People claim you should create a Kratky system, set it & forget it. Plants are permitted to do their own activities before time to harvest. That is a bit true because Kratky is an entirely passive system. No electrical power is used, and no pumps and wicks are required.

2. Fogponics

Fogponics may be described as a working fog. In its simplest sense, the growers use fog to grow the plants in the fogponic method. The fogponic system, like the humid environment present in the rainforest, uses special foggers (electrical) to pump & vibrate in pressure to turn the nutrient plus water combination into humidity.

It produces a persistent humid and nutrient-rich atmosphere for plant roots. For fogponics, the root system may have full coverage since the tiny droplet scale of the gravity-defying fog will move and invade the space around it. Plants are provided with what they need, soil, nutrients, oxygen just like any other successful hydroponic system. As in the soil counterparts, they don't have to look for these acts. All their actions are expended on rising, planting, or sprouting (for seedlings), and on root (cloning) growth. However, unlike traditional hydroponics, where plants are oxygenated by an air pump from the water, Fogponics/Aeroponics works by having the plants in the air. It's a tray/foam catch. The plant roots are expelled; thus, they have plenty of access to oxygen. The plants supply water via the foggers. In general, the action is automated by a timer. Fogponics works just like the aeroponics. But instead, the foggers are used to spray the water. They create and atomize droplets that are much smaller than in aeroponics, typically fewer than 10 microns in size.

3. The Dutch Bucket System

NFT channels are designed to grow small leaf crops like lettuce and small herbs, but it is challenging to grow bigger plants like tomatoes, cucumbers, beans, and peppers in NFT channels.

Large plants are typically more of a "long-term" plant and require more root area than an NFT channel provides (they can also capsize the channels), and hydroponics (many very big growers use hanging gutters & Rockwool slabs).

But, for a smaller grower without all the sensors and alarms, those Rockwool slabs might dry out if the injection system collapsed or just didn't feed in any way. It's really hard to fully "re-wet" it. Even if you cover it with water, the moist region around the roots will continue to just wet. The water follows the easiest route and easily passes over and around the surface.

That's bad because the roots would not branch out in the dry areas as the plants keep growing. One of the main reasons we use Bato Bucket Systems and materials is the fact that it is simple to re-wet perlite and another is the reservoir at the bottom of the bucket which holds some stockpile nutrient in situation power goes off or whether the plant requires some more nutrient that day because it is extra sunny. The elbows and excess that are bato bucket's part protect the plants from having their roots drowned too much nutrient they required because there wasn't that much sun, and the day was cold, and the plant didn't take up as much as they were feeding. We just find that Bato Buckets are far more user-friendly. We are using bato buckets as farmers are using bigger containers called "Dutch" or Bato buckets. These buckets are loaded with growing material; usually, perlite and nutrients stream into the bucket through a tube to hold Perlite moist. The waste stream is also not recirculated as the plants will stay in all of these buckets for up to a year, and recirculation of nutrients could transfer contaminants from one plant to the other.

Chapter 3: Hydroponics Farming

Hydroponic farming enables us to grow plants utilizing solutions of mineral nutrients, in water, without soil. The hydroponic farmer regulates nutrient composition in the liquid solution that is used to water the crops. He/she also controls the amount the plants are supplied with nutrients. The hydroponic grower clearly manages the plants growing environment. The system is highly advanced but still needs to be managed well. As previously stated, the mechanism is managed and not simply operated. Therefore, water-efficient and nutrient-efficient delivered straight to the plant's root structure. Since water and nutrient rates are monitored, these components are distributed at the required levels and whenever needed. Water and nutrients combined lead to success and growth rate.

In the production of crops, the lighting aspect is also important. This is accomplished by planting out into vertical frameworks where sunlight is maximized while minimizing plant density, crowding, and shading. Hydroponic farming of the present-day follows the 3-D method and is developed vertically within multilevel growing fields. So now, in terms of minerals, water, and light, we have perfect growing conditions, combined with the ability to expand vertically. It contributes to the yield of each unit area significantly, as the hydroponic garden is no longer 2-D, but it has become a 3-D model and architecture. It maximizes the real growing area & utilizes what fields of restricted planting conditions might have been unused.

3.1 Why Use Hydroponics?

Below are stated some reasons why hydroponics should be used:

• The capacity to generate yields higher than conventional soil-based agriculture.

• Enabling food to be grown as well as consumed in regions of the world that are unable to support crops in soil.

• Eliminate the need for massive use of pesticides (considering that most pests stay in the soil); effectively start cleaning up our air, water, soil, and food.

• Products free of pesticides via biological pest control or control methods approved by OMRI.

• Recycling or re-use of nutrient solutions in other areas, such as pot plants & turf management.

• Growing mediums are reusable and recyclable.

• It may need less space depending on the type of hydroponics used, thereby enabling for a higher density of plants in the same area.

• There is easy facilitation of non-arable land.

• Potential to grow all year.

• It Fosters general awareness of our climate.

• The closed recirculation system allows nutrient solution to be managed by the grower and thus exactly which nutrients the plants obtain.

• Differing nutrient formulae at different stages to meet different plants.

• Routine nutrient testing assures that all components are present at the concentrations they need. Unnecessary build-ups of undesired amounts of nutrients, like nitrites, could be avoided.

• Hydroponic plants are much more resistant to the pests.

• Control over external factors translates into a product that is nutritionally superior, i.e., vegetable product.

• It eliminates the use of artificial ripening products & pesticides used for imported products.

• Good taste and much better than its counterparts in the soil.

• Not harmful to the environment.

There are a number of causes for using hydroponics to cultivate fresh food, from our body's wellbeing to environmental safety. Hydroponics prevents plant and soil-borne pests as well as disease, and the usage of large amounts of pesticides is not necessary. This, in turn, lessens soil erosion, as well as pollution from air and water. Traditional soil-based agriculture causes pesticides to run off into rivers and streams, damaging fish populations. Reducing pollution is important for the conservation of natural plants and animals in areas near to crops. Integrated Pest Management, or IPM, is a quite popular form of insect pests & disease control in the hydroponics. IPM is a program used by farmers to closely monitor insect species, utilizing biological controls or pest management approaches approved by OMRI. Biological controls involve releasing beneficial insects such as ladybugs or lacewing larvae, for exploiting threats such as aphids or whiteflies.

Conservation & preservation are a major part of growing hydroponics. In recirculating systems, hydroponic nutrient solutions are filtered and may be used again in other gardening areas such as potted plants or lawn areas. You will sterilize and re-use several forms of growing media inside your hydroponic system. Inert media such as coconut coir, perlite, and grow stones are built for excellent water absorption and the diffusion of air so they can be re-used in potted plants or soil gardens. Such materials are re-used and processed to reduce the amount of pollution that ends up in the water.

Hydroponics offers places to the world with low or infertile lands hope for food growth. This offers exposure to produce for communities of people in these regions safely. The vegetables produced in these regions, and other locations with hydroponic systems, are fresh, tasty, and full of flavor-much more so than their equivalents in the soil. Hydroponics empowers populations who might otherwise have little exposure to nutritious or even healthy foods.

The hydroponic system is the way to go, from a scientific point of view. Closed, recirculating programs allow for full control of the nutrient solution so that growers can know exactly which nutrients their plants are getting. Different nutrient formulations are specially designed to suit different plant types at various stages of growth. Growers may choose the nutrients depending on the crop they cultivate, and they can change the formula to the planting or flowering stage, which results in higher yields than conventional soil-based agriculture. Obviously, healthy plants are more resistant to pests than damaged or unhealthy plants or plants which do not get sufficient nutrients.

Additionally, nutrient meters may be used to check the concentration of nutrients daily. Tests enable growers to introduce elements if they see any indication of a deficiency in nutrients. It means that all components are available at appropriate concentrations, allowing for optimum conditions of growth suited to the specific needs of each plant.

Objects which are not included in goods produced hydroponically are almost as worth noting as items present. Soil removal ensures excessive build-ups with toxic mineral concentrations can be prevented. Nutrient toxicity is almost as essential to plants as nutrient deficiency, so hydroponics will effectively avoid both of these.

Food grown near the distribution point decreases the transport costs and the use of fuel as well. Ignoring imported produce ensures that the user does not absorb chemical products or pesticides to grow. To protect our health and preserving the natural flavor of the food, this is essential. Vertical systems like Ez Gro need less volume, which enables plant density to be very large in one location. By not using up so much room, when they have unused land, growers have the liberty to do what they want. They can raise more crops, or they could use their property for other reasons. Growing further food in a small area can even contribute to the land being able to return to its normal, unfragmented condition. This is indeed a big step in animal population conservation, as we can rebuild their habitats. The effect of environmental factors often decreases with hydroponics. It translates into the capacity to grow outstanding vegetables throughout the year!

Hydroponic development has so many advantages. It just seems like the ideal choice. Hydroponics fosters a general awareness of our climate. By raising the traditional agriculture pollution, it can even help to protect the atmosphere. Hydroponically grown foods taste better, and have high nutrients inside, rendering them better than that of the alternative. This environmentally friendly food production approach is needed to support the growing population of our world and will be the future's preferred method of farming.

3.2 Hydroponics vs. Aquaponics

Hydroponics and aquaponics are at the pioneers of soilless technologies, each giving growers several significant benefits for growing plants while reducing potentially hazardous environmental effects.

What is Hydroponics?

Hydroponics is a process used for thousands of years to grow plants without soil. At first, growing plants without any soil may seem confusing, but hydroponics is a complicated system that works well over the conventional method of growing plants in soil. There are two elements they need for plants to grow: a collection of essential plants, nutrients & water. Because of this, when the nutrients are supplied in the water and distributed to the roots, there is no need in the growth system to have soil present. A nutrient-charged, aquatic solution is filtered via the root zone in a hydroponic growing system to get the plants with the support they need for maximum growth. The use of hydroponic growing systems has many advantages: fewer resources are used, no arable land is required, and the harvestable plants are of high quality than when they are produced using traditional methods. Such benefits have increased the use of hydroponics over the past 60 to 70 years and widened the restricted indoor & urban gardening opportunities.

What is Aquaponics?

Aquaponics is another innovative plant-growing method with no soil to sustain the root systems, which is slightly different from hydroponics. Aquaponics is a mixture of hydroponic growing plants and aquaculture (fish raising) technique.

Just like in hydroponics, plants are produced in a soilless climate in an aquaponics method. Instead of plants receiving their nutrients through soil sources, an aquatic solution delivers the essential nutrients directly to the roots required for plant growth, where effective nutrient uptake may

occur.

In aquaponics, the fish provide such a natural source of organic nutrients from their excreted wastes; beneficial microbes transform the waste into useful plant nutrient sources; the plants in effect automatically filter the water, supplying the fish and microbes with a clean-living climate.

Similarities between Hydroponics & Aquaponics

Because aquaponics is the mix of hydroponic and aquaculture principles, it's logical that the two methods have several similarities that render them both useful.

1. Longer Growing Period than Conventional Gardening

That might be one of the most appealing similarities here between two schemes. Most hydroponics & aquaponics systems are housed indoors, are sheltered from the atmosphere, and have external lights to expand. For this, plants can be grown even longer than the period permits outside.

2. Lessened Harmful Impacts on the Environment.

Indoor plants have a much lower likelihood of insect and weeds pressure. This lower pressure is a clear result of a system that is contained and cannot be infested due to soil movement, wind, pest migration, etc. Weed seeds on wind or planting implements are also not spread by birds or transferred from the garden bed to the garden bed. Lower pest, as well as weed pressure, means fewer pesticide treatments, which could possibly have adverse impacts on the environment.

Although in both processes, plants are grown specifically in water. They use less water than traditional cultivation because the aquatic methods are recirculated as well as re-used. The aquaponics utilizes about 10% of the water used in soil gardening.

3. Plants Tend to Grow Much Faster

Plants that are grown in soilless structures grow 30-50% faster on average than plants cultivated straight into the soil. The reasoning behind the rapid growth is due to additional nutrients in an aquatic solution at the surface. Such extra oxygen encourages the root growth as well as facilitates smoother and more effective absorption of nutrients. You may put the energy saved into faster growth.

4. Yields Higher

On average, plants that are grown in soilless structures produce more than conventional growth methods by about 30-40%. This is partly due to proper monitoring of nutrients in aquatic solutions, ensuring that plants achieve optimal levels of fertilizer, but also reduced disease as well as insect pressure, as well as more fine-tuned growing conditions.

Differences in Hydroponics and Aquaponics

Although there are some similarities among hydroponics and aquaponics, introducing fish to the aquaponics systems causes certain distinctions that are worth mentioning and acknowledge when developing a soilless growing method.

1. Design of the Systems and Its Components

Among the biggest differences in nature in the depths of the expected grow beds. Typically, hydroponics uses 6 "deep growing beds because roots can spread easily in the aquatic solution with very little root compaction concern. Aquaponics needs at least 12 "deep growing beds to enable the fish to swim around within their surroundings.

The next difference is due to the varying materials. Hydroponics systems are quite sterile, and no growing external media are required to support the root systems or plants.

On the other side, aquaponics requires an environment along with its core to host the helpful micro-organisms. To help the plant/root hydroponics system, hydroponics does not need deep grow media. Some Hydroponic structures do not even use growing materials.

2. Startup Cost/Speed

The startup costs between both the hydroponics & aquaponics systems are quite close, irrespective of the fish. For the microbes to live in, the aquaponics system requires to grow media, which brings a little additional startup expense. The major difference, however, is the cost of buying fish to inventory the grow beds in aquaponics. The costs of fish vary according to the variety you choose to produce and how much you need it. A big difference between the two methods resides in the start speeds. Upon installing a hydroponics system, it's only essential to allow the nutrient solution process to settle before introducing plants for a few days at the most. Due to the fish, aquaponic systems are slower to get up and run. Creation of the nitrifying bacteria required to break away the fish waste takes at least a month; certain processes will take up to 3 months to maintain the environment sufficiently add plants.

3. Running Costs

Every machine has one running cost, different from the other. Hydroponic systems require fertilizers that are obtained throughout the growing season to keep the nutrient solution replenish able. Aquaponics does have a higher cost of electricity since the system needs a higher oxygenation level in the water to sustain the fish. The operating costs for aquaponics, in general, are somewhat more costly.

4. Plants

Hydroponic growing systems could be used for plants with higher nutrient requirements since the nutrient solution can be modified to suit plant needs; aquaponic systems usually work best to assist plants with lower nutrient requirements like lettuce, other leafy greens, as well as herbs.

5. Ecosystem

An ecosystem is a group of organisms that produces the resulting climate. Hydroponics cannot be regarded as an ecosystem, while aquaponics can be called an ecosystem because of the interaction of plant/fish/microbe.

Misconception & Myths

Myth: "Aquaponics is Less Costly."

One point theoretically received by prospective farmers is that aquaponics is a simpler method to run than hydroponics. Although fish food is generally cheaper than nutrient alternatives, it is also used in larger quantities, and typically has to be combined with other nutrient supplements not present in the feed itself. If you rely on this to have one or the other, you should make detailed cost analyses and comparisons.

Myth: Aquaponics= More Sales, Since You could Sell the Fish

One misleading myth concerning aquaponic financing is that there is an additional income source of fish sales for aquaponic growers. Competing with other fishery producers and finding customers ready to pay higher prices for fish is very difficult. Effective fish processing needs vigorous breeding techniques that need more equipment and space than an aquaponic system.

Myth: "Hydroponics is Boring."

Don't let this statement fool you! Just because hydroponics doesn't include live organisms, it doesn't make it boring. It's rewarding to run a farm of every kind. Hydroponic farmers are happy with growing & harvesting special and unique crops and maintaining a growing area!

Find the Technique that Fits your System

Choosing a growth strategy that will support you is important. We find that most growers want to continue with hydroponics as their key growth strategy, whereas aquaponics is generally best adapted to smaller or special niches in marketing. Hydroponics is used to a greater extent by both hobbyists and commercial growers. It's easy to predict that just because hydroponics is easier to run, it looks much better indoors, costs less, and has more & faster ROI (Return on Investment) most significantly.

3.3 Hydroponic Grow Mediums

The growing medium, in hydroponics, takes the place of dirt/soil. Not providing nutrients, but also that the roots may support the weight of the plants and keep it upright. It is possible to use almost every inert substance as a growing medium. Inert means it can't/won't rot or decompose quickly, thereby supplying plants with nutrients. Hydroponic growth media is simply a soilless, usually porous medium that can retain the moisture & oxygen which the root system needs to expand. Non-porous substances can also be used, but it would need to be more regular to use no growing medium at certain watering cycles so that the roots do not dry out among watering.

The growing medium will be unable to produce anything by itself. If you put plants in hydroponic grow media and watered them with plain water, a nutritional deficiency will cause the plants to starve. It's just there to continue supporting both the weight of the plants and the nutrients & oxygen the roots require. The nutrients required by the plants are supplied by the nutrient solution and are watered and moistened by the growing media.

Rockwool, Coconut fiber/Coconut chips, Lightweight Expanded Clay Aggregate (called Hydro corn or Grow Rock), and Perlite or Vermiculite are some of the most commonly used growing material. While there are many materials that can be used in hydroponics as rising media, they could all have unique properties than other media types. We even see the use of hay bales as a growth medium for growing tomatoes, using drop lines on the upper edge to drip the nutrient solution on to the roots of hay bales and tomato plants. There is not one growing media that is greater than the others. Eventually, though, many growers prefer one type over another. In deciding what to be used as a growing media, there are lots of things to remember. Your growing-in type of system and how you build and design the framework is the main factor.

Although no one has the right to grow media for all circumstances, some growing media work in different structures better than others. The target is still the same with any hydroponic system and with any form of that media. You just have to have the roots clean, neither soggy nor sticky. If the rising environment becomes soggy and polluted, the seeds may suffocate from a lack of oxygen. This condition will easily lead to dying roots and root decay.

Things to consider for each form of the hydroponic system regarding every grow media

1. Drip Systems

Drip systems are relatively easy to handle the humidity in. As long as you plan it so that it has good drainage, and you should be able to maintain through media from being too soggy to restrict water pooling at the edge. We like using river rock at the base to aid runoff and prevent the rising media from sitting down in a pool of water.

2. NFT Systems

At the bottom of a river where the roots wick away moisture, NFT systems use a very small, yet steady stream of water. Most NFT systems use either tiny starter cubes or tiny1-inch buckets, and just let the roots literally drop down into the water. If all these cubes or baskets are near to the supply of water, the rising media will quickly become saturated, and the combination will contribute to "stem rot" when the growing media all over the stem is often saturated.

3. Ebb-Flow (Flood and Drain) Systems

The construction of flood & drain systems may vary significantly in design. But basically, you'd want to stay far away from any that media like Perlite & Vermiculite floating about. Every time the machine turns on, the growing media is weightless for the flooding stage, so the plants may drop all their strength and still want to tip over. Based on your system, you could reduce the amount of flood, so floating is low as long as the root ball could still get more than enough moisture and that you don't lose plant support. Plant support cannot be as much of a concern if plants of the form of growing vine such as strawberries, peas, or melons which would be attached to the trellis.

For flood and drain systems, because depending on the type of growing media, you want to make sure that you should have good drainage so that the growing media is not saturated constantly.

Grow rocks aren't going to pick up a lot of moisture, but we like to use cocoa chips a lot because they're affordable, but coco chips wick up water when they're lying in it. So, at the edge, a sheet of river rock prevents it from lying in the water.

4. Water Culture Systems

Water culture systems generally don't use much of any growing media, because they are built to submerge the plant roots in the nutrient solution itself. But normally plants are started with small starter cubes as well as small buckets. Usually, starter cubes are held above the waterline, while baskets may stay either just above or below the waterline. The growing medium you select and the amount of moisture it consumes can make a significant difference. You do not want it to be sticky; you want to have it down to be warm, and the surface must be dry. The roots of the nutrient solution must grow downwards.

Now you might ask if it's so big of an issue if that media gets polluted, why the roots won't get suffocated if they're in a water culture system, i.e., all the time underwater. Not all crops do well in structures for water cultures. Next and most notably, an air compressor is used by a water culture system to produce lots of air bubbles to the underwater base. The plants specifically get oxygen from all these air bubbles, and also the air bubbles raise the amount of dissolved oxygen in the water itself.

5. Aeroponic Systems

Usually, aeroponic systems do not use much that grows media. Aeroponic systems are built to encourage the roots to hang in the air, although often misted with a nutrient solution to prevent the roots from drying out. Seeds are begun in any small starter cubes or small buckets, and then when they actually plan in the aeroponic method, then they're wide enough.

You would like to ensure they don't saturate the cubes or grow media in the bins. Although almost all the roots can remain in the air with no risk of becoming suffocated, moist growing media will contribute to "stem rot" around the steam plants.

6. Wick Systems

Wick systems are indeed the least-used sort of system, but without moving parts, engines, or pumps, they focus on wicking up moisture via a piece of fabric into the growing media as well as roots to the plants. You'll need to use a growing media with wick systems that absorb and quickly hold onto humidity. Using a wick larger/wider, or more than one, you will restrict the amount of water flowing to the plant.

Different Types of Growing Media Hydroponically

1. Rockwool: Rockwool is among the most widely used hydroponic grow media Rockwool is a pure, porous, non-degradable material consisting primarily of granite or limestone, which is super-heated and melted and woven into thin fibers such as cotton candy. Then the Rockwool shapes into bricks, boards slabs, cubes, or flocking. Rockwool quickly sucks up water, so you'll need to be cautious not to let it get saturated, or it might suffocate the roots of your plants, as well as contribute to stem rotting and root rotting. Before use, Rockwool must be evened up with pH. That is achieved by soaking it before use in pH balanced water.

2. Grow Rock (Hydrocorn): It is lightweight, expanded clay aggregate (L.E.C.A.), which is a form of clay that is super-fired to produce a porous texture. It's strong enough to provide stable protection for plants but still low weight.

Grow rocks are an un-degradable, sterile growing medium that retains moisture, has a favorable pH and wicks up the nutrient solution to your plant's root systems. Hydrocorn growing media can be re-used, washed, sterilized, and then re-used again. Though it may be very time-consuming to clean and sterilize large quantities of growing rocks on a massive scale. Grow Rock is among the most common growing media used for hydroponics, and it is held more than almost every store that sells hydroponic supplies.

3. Coco Chips/Coco Fiber: "Coco coir" (Coconut fiber) originates from the outer coconut husk. What has once deemed a waste commodity among the best available medium? While coco coir is an organic material, it starts to break down and decomposes quite gradually, making it ideal for hydroponics, so it will not provide further nutrients to the plants that grow therein. Coco coir, however, is pH neutral, keeps very well in the rain, yet still enables good ventilation for the roots. Coco fiber appears in two varieties, coco coir (fiber), and coco chips. They're mostly made up of husks of coconut; the only distinction is the size of the particle. The particle size of the coco fiber is about the same as that of the potting soil, while the particle size of the coco chips is just like small wood chips. 4. **Perlite**: Perlite consists mainly of minerals that are exposed to a very high heat, which further spread it like popcorn so that it becomes very light, porous and absorbent. Perlite is very porous and also has a neutral pH, outstanding wicking motion. Perlite can either be used alone or combined with other can medium types. Nonetheless, since perlite is so lightweight that it floats, based on how you built the hydroponic system, perlite alone might not be the best option to grow media for flood & drain systems.

5. Vermiculite: It is a silicate mineral that expands when subjected to very high heat, just like perlite.

Vermiculite is rather similar to perlite as a growing medium, except it has a fairly high potential for cation-exchange, meaning it can retain nutrients for later usage. Vermiculite is also very light like perlite, which appears to float. There are various uses and forms of vermiculite, so you'll need to make sure that what you will get is intended for use in horticulture. To be sure, the easiest way is to get to a nursery.

6. Oasis Cubes: Oasis Cubes are identical to cubes of Rockwool, and also have similar characteristics. Yet oasis cubes are much like the stiff white and green floral foam used by forests in their flower shows to keep the stems hold. Oasis cubes are such an open-cell medium that ensures the cells are able to absorb air and water. Throughout the substance, the open cells wick moisture, and the roots can spread and develop quickly via the open cell framework. Although oasis cubes are typically to use as starter cubes for plants grown hydroponically, they also have bags that you can fill the growing containers with. While oasis cubes are similar to Rockwool, they do not become waterlogged as quickly as Rockwool cubes do. And so, don't let it be in regular contact with water supply or you will still have waterlogging problems.

7. Growstone Hydroponic Substrate: Growstones are made of glass, which is recycled. They are identical to grow rocks (hydro corn) yet are composed of clay and marbles. Growstones are low weight, unevenly formed, porous & reusable, supplying root zone with strong aeration & moisture. They have excellent wicking power and can wick up to 4 inches of water above the surface. You'll need to make sure the drainage is sufficient or full enough so that it doesn't wick water up to the top. However, as with the growing media in any hydroponic system, if the surface of the growing media is constantly moist, you may have stem rot issues. While they're made of recycled glass, they're not sharp, and even if they crack, you won't get cut from it.

8. Sand: Sand is probably a common hydroponic grow material. It is the main growing media used in the Florida Hydroponic Greenhouse Epcot Center. Mainly for the large trees and plants which are grown hydroponically. Sand is just like Rock, just smaller in size. Due to the smaller particle size than standard Rock, moisture may not drain out as quickly. Additionally, sand is usually blended with Vermiculite, Perlite, and coco coir. Both help maintains moisture and also support the roots by aerating the mix.

3.4 Hydroponic Nutrient Guide and Grow Lights

What Plant Needs to Grow and Survive, Plants Need?

- Oxygen
- Carbon Dioxide
- Lights
- Water
- Nutrients

Plants for respiration receive oxygen & carbon dioxide from the atmosphere. Lights provide energy to plants, which is used for making food in the photosynthesis cycle. They may receive lights from the sun's natural lighting, or artificial lights from growing lamps. Water provides moisture to plants. Nutrients present in the water are something the soilless growers are also in total control to enable plants to reach their full growth potential. These are what we're going to start talking about.

Macronutrients

Macronutrients, as the name indicates, are the ones growing plants need to have in large quantities.

-Nitrogen (N)

Nitrogen is the main plant-growing food, especially the stage of vegetative growth. No nitrogen, no leaves. Essentially, in leaf and stem growth, it plays a crucial role.

-Phosphorus (P)

Phosphorus is essential to photosynthesis, which is one of the elements of DNA, the plant genetic memory unit that participates in seed production as well as plant vigor. In the initial stage of seedling, germination and flowering, plants require Phosphorus throughout in relatively large amounts. So, it's liable for the development of:

- Seeds
- Roots
- Flowering
- Fruits

-Potassium (K)

Potassium is used at all phases of the growth of plants. This aids in the production of starch, sugars, as well as carbohydrates. It also performs some role in the stem, roots, and flower growth. Plants with enough Potassium have high resistance to bacteria as well as insects.

-Calcium (Ca)

Fast-growing flowers and vegetables need Ca almost as much as their macronutrients. This is important for the creation and development of cells.

-Magnesium (Mg)

Again, plants that are fast-growing also need large amounts of Mg. Mg is important for the development of chlorophyll. This works by photosynthesizing to produce oxygen and is noticeable in healthy and strong plants.

-Sulfur (S)

Sulfur the elements of 21 protein-forming amino acids, other hormones, and vitamins like vitamin B.

Micronutrients

Lesser amounts of micronutrients are needed. Today, they play a significant role in the growth of plants.

-Zinc (Zn)

Zincs function for the production of chlorophyll with other materials. It is essential for stem development, and critical stimulus for enzymes in most plants.

-Manganese (Mn)

Mn assists in the use of nitrogen along with iron in chlorophyll development.

-Iron (Fe)

Needed for synthesis of chlorophyll and is essential to the enzyme process.

-Boron (Bo)

It can be merged with calcium in the development of cell membranes as well as chlorophyll.

These are a full list of micronutrients. But first, take better care of the macronutrients, and don't let the plants become too depleted and wasteful of those micronutrients, and you're going excellently. But, it's not enough to get to learn all the essential resources the plants require. In fact, certain nutrients are soluble at multiple pH levels, which will go into specifics.

Why Do Plants Need Light?

Plants require food for survival. They're not actively looking for the foods like the human, though. Rather, through a process known as photosynthesis, they use sunlight to produce food (sugars).

Plants store the energy of the sunlight in their leaves' green pigment, called chlorophyll.

Types of Grow Lights

There's a huge variety of sizes and types when we talk about grow lights. But in the end, the three main categories-High-Intensity Discharge (HID), LED Fluorescent, and Fluorescent. This may be the most popular option for home growers, mainly due to its quality, its acceptable performance. There are two Fluorescent lights forms -CFL and Tube style lights.

1. CFL (Compact Fluorescent Lights)

CFL Bulb

CFL lights are the cheap twisty bulbs which can be located anywhere near your home. Because they are tiny and don't generate much heat, they could be located near plants and thus are perfect bulbs for small installations.

2. Tube-Style Fluorescent Lights

There are many different types, such as T5, T8, T12, T5 lights, amongst them, are the most commonly used and the most efficient. They are much larger than CFLs and are typically placed in a row with many bulbs organized paralleled one another.

3. HID (High-Intensity Discharge)

HID lamps are better than fluorescent ones. They offer more lights as well as more heat per watt. But they start to get hot fast as well as require a lot of ventilation.

4. HPS (High-Pressure Sodium)

HPS Light

High-pressure sodium bulbs in the yellow and red portion of the spectrum provide more glow. Although they may be used in all growth phases of plants, they may be favored towards the fruiting and flowering plants.

5. MH (Metal Halide)

MH emits the light at the spectrum's blue range. Therefore, it is better suited for plant vegetation.

6. CMH (Ceramic Metal Halide)

Ceramic Metal Halide (CMH) light bulbs seem like MH, but it functions quite efficiently and quite differently. CMH has a much larger luminosity than MH & HPS. And it has a life-span better than the two.

7. The LED (Light Emitting Diode)

Led Lights

LED lights eventually come later to the indoor gardening. As compared to other lights, it's such an efficient method. They produce a lot of light with a minimal amount of electricity. LED's are extremely lightweight. They run nice and usually have a built-in cooling system out of the box. LEDs consist of many diodes, and growers may configure the light wavelength/ light hues they want for plants. LEDs are costly as well as they generally take up lots of space.

Grow Light Buyer Tips

If you're total beginners and your systems are small, then CFLs are really a great choice. They are comparatively cheap and offer enough light to expand smaller, stealthier regions. CFLs work perfectly for small plants that need little light.

Would you like a better solution for each growing phase for your plants? You should stick to the lights with HPs/MH. For the vegetative as well as other stages, MH/CMH lights are used, while HPs are used for the flowering process.

If your budget is not a concern, and you want something new, durable, energy-efficient, go with LED lights of the length spectrum. In addition to the weather that gives your growing system great heat, growing lights have become the primary cause that raises the temperature of your system.

You'll have to have some forms of ventilation in that situation. If your budget is high, consider having a water chiller to ensure the best growth condition for your plants.

3.5 What to grow hydroponically?

In hydroponics, you can grow everything provided by building a proper system and providing plants with appropriate nutritional content. But you really shouldn't take that attitude and grow whatever you want. This is because, in hydroponics, certain plants can grow perfectly well, while others will not generate planned yields. Many plants need you to thrive, at the same time, for their proper care and deployment. It's better to start with something simple and thrives in hydroponics first, to offer some suggestions for beginners. Let's all go to this list.

Flowers: Growing flowers adapt perfectly to hydroponic gardening as they can grow in greater numbers and can be grown throughout the year. Some flowers would do well in a hydroponic garden, so flowers can be cut or transplanted when the seedlings are big enough.

Herbs: In a hydroponic environment, a ton of herbs can grow very well. Anise, basil, catnip, chervil, chives, cilantro, coriander, fennel, lavender, dill, marjoram, mint, parsley, rosemary, garlic, oregano, tarragon, and thyme are some of the better do.

Watercress: A part of the mustard tribe, low-growing as well as trailing European perennial. It develops easily from seed. The normal season lasts from mid-autumn to spring. The leaves get too graded in taste to be edible after their flower buds emerge. In a hydroponic system, it's also easy to grow indoors. Begin seed plants by gently sowing them in pots packed with a liquid. The watercress has many cooking, medical, and decorative uses.

Vegetables: Artichokes, tomatoes, kale, spinach, cabbage, asparagus, broccoli, beets, cauliflower, Brussels sprouts, and peas are all vegetables that do very well in a hydroponic garden. Hydroponic plants, such as onions, carrots, parsnips, cabbage, yams, and radishes, will also thrive under the soil but may require additional care. Grass, zucchini, and vining plants are some varieties to avoid. They could be grown in a hydroponic garden, but they are not effective in volume, and they are simply not practical. They could overwhelm the entire unit. It is better to spend the money on crops more suitable for compact systems.

Cool Season Crops:

- Broccoli and cauliflower
- Cabbage and bok choy
- Lettuces
- Peas, snow peas, and sugar snaps
- Green onions
- Spinach
- Carrots

Warm Season Crops:

- Green peppers
- Eggplants
- Tomatoes
- Green beans
- Cucumbers
- Squash
- Melons

Top 10 Fruits and Vegetables to Grow Hydroponically:

Hydroponics is a plant-growing system in water and without soil. At optimal levels, minerals & nutrients are provided to the water so that the plants can commit their resources to grow vegetables and fruit, resulting in greater production. You can produce anything using the hydroponics. In a hydroponic greenhouse, here are our top ten fruits and veggies to grow:

- Tomatoes
- Lettuce
- Cucumber
- Spring Onion
- Peppers
- Spinach
- Strawberries
- Blueberries
- Basil
- Coriander

What Should You not Grow First?

It does not imply that you couldn't cultivate these kinds of plants. They're just difficult to grow and may need special attention. Even the results aren't as nice as in the soils. Nevertheless, if you want to try to discover the specific plants that you want to cultivate the most exciting, or if you're professional growers, don't skip them.

Deep Root crops: For the root systems, certain root plants require tons of depth. You will have to help the seeds, as well as the medium, has to be deep enough and wide enough to grow the roots. Such plants contain potatoes, carrots, and turnips.

A large plant that requires spaces: If you lack the spaces to grow, you can stay away from the melons, pumpkins, corn, and squash. What's more, the crops are heavy enough, so you need to support them properly. Even if you have such a large area as a greenhouse, the barrier is removed.

Chapter 4: Indoor and Outdoor Hydroponics

The environment is warm enough in many areas to enable outdoor hydroponics systems to grow planting crops for a long portion of the year, if not the whole year-with some good management techniques and adequate crop selection, of course. With an environmentally-controlled greenhouse, you will run close to indoor gardens, except that ideally, you might get lots of free light as well as quick exchanges of air to keep the hydroponic crop happy and healthy above the root system. When you cultivate indoors using grow lights, you can garden in your hydroponics system year-round-being able to successfully grow just about any type of plant to maturity irrespective of what the outside season is.

We have to; therefore, focus on areas such as lighting, whether normal or from growing lights, as well as the value of a good environment for the plant's green and flowering sections. What about the hydroponics system itself-can you use an outdoor hydroponics system-and what or how do you need to do differently to make it work outdoors just about as well as indoors under the lights? Let's have a look at the comprehensive Indoor & Outdoor Hydroponics overview.

4.1 Indoor Hydroponics

There are several good reasons that hydroponic gardening usually takes place indoors. The increased control of an indoor or greenhouse environment is ideal to reap all the benefits of hydroponic growth. The benefits of hydroponic gardening typically involve faster growth rates and greater yields due to increased nutrient and oxygen accessibility (for the roots) of the plant.

The use of hydroponics was reported as far back as the first century when Roman Emperor Tiberius became known as the transparent stone for off-season cucumbers. Indoor hydroponic systems can be built of items like a 5-gallon container with a lid, a pot, a growing medium, air stone, and an aquarium pump. Studies showed that hydroponics plants grow up to 30% to 40% faster and have a higher yield than a plant in the soil. Hydroponics helps plants to survive in areas where no soil exists, or the soil is polluted, such as rooftops, derelict buildings, barren urban lands, etc. Weeding is not required; water consumption is up to 10 times lower, and indoor hydroponic systems reduce access to pests and other insects. Home hydroponics systems are of two types.

The passive hydroponic system depends on the capillary impact or what is often called the wicking effect. The capillary effect leads to the uplifting of nutrient-rich material. The fluid is formed and consumed by the growing medium in a passive hydroponic system.

An active hydroponic system depends on a pump to deliver the nutrient solution to the roots, and any excess solution will simply drain away. In an active system, a growing medium is not needed.

Hydroponic farming allows us to grow in places or in times where the typical cultivation of plants outside the soil is impossible.

Building an Indoor Hydroponic System

While there are many various forms that can be taken by an indoor hydroponic system, they all work in the same manner and have the same possible benefits and problems.

The type that you end up with will rely on how much and what kind of space you have, what kind of lighting you have, what equipment and resources you have, how much you want to spend, and how careful you are with DIY projects.

Since the basic hydroponic procedure is the same, you can create whatever modifications you want to enhance upon the basic design once you understand it.

Whether you're building a system by yourself or purchasing a kit, these are usually the components you'll need along with plants and maintenance supplies:

- A reservoir for the liquid. (water/nutrient)
- An aquarium-type water pump and circulation hose.
- An aquarium aerator.
- LED grow-lights for the dark side.
- Some kind of structure for carrying pots
- Opaque containers for plant roots

Key to Success

The key to success in an indoor hydroponic garden is to be able to fully know and then simply meet the requirements of your plants. It applies especially to the lighting and feeding requirements of various plants. A lettuce crop can do well grown under fluorescent lights, while tomatoes and other vegetables need a much more intense light source to ensure strong and healthy growth. Each plant has a preferred pH in conjunction with nutrient strength and light intensity. It is also very normal for your plants to adjust the light demands and nutritional requirements as they grow. They may need, for example, a dark photoperiod to get them to maturity, or they may need less nitrogen and more phosphorus and potassium as they switch from vegetative growth to flowering/fruiting.

It's extremely helpful to have a feeding schedule that is adapted to the needs of the plants you cultivate beforehand. Once you have a feeding schedule, it's only a matter of keeping your nutrient solution balanced on a daily basis.

Indoor organic and hydroponic gardening can be very worthwhile, but for the beginner, the challenges presented by the interior plants can be daunting, and even an accomplished gardener can face challenges.

4.2 Outdoor Hydroponics

Although indoor conditions make it easier to monitor many of the variables influencing how a hydroponic system works, many farmers are also pursuing outdoor hydroponic gardening. In reality, with a few modifications, most outdoor hydroponic systems can offer many of the same benefits to farmers as an indoor environment. Outdoor hydroponic systems are also an alternative to countries affected by poverty that lack food security due to lack of resources.

Outdoor hydroponics provides you the ideal balance of nutrients and water, and the plants can thrive even better and faster in the summer when there is enough sunshine than in the soil gardens. In a soilless outdoor hydroponic system, not only will your plants grow quicker and safer, but you won't need to weed them, or struggle with insects that can decimate your plants.

If you're not fully sure where to start, here are some clear guidelines to ensure that your outdoor growing box gets right.

Fundamentals of Outdoor Hydroponics

Some of the fundamentals for outdoor hydroponics include treating plants as if they are in conventional soil-based systems— except that they only get their nutrients differently. For conventional gardens, you need to design the way you would. The only difference is that you have to think about what's in the soil, instead of thinking about what's in the hydroponic nutrients.

Natural Light

Outdoor hydroponics is very exciting in one major way. This means that in hydroponic, you do not need to worry about grow lights. For a few years, manufacturers have made great strides in hydroponic growing lights, making them nourish plants with different luminosity and light spectrum, but nothing really substitutes for the power of the sun. The plants are submerged in direct sunlight to induce vibrant photosynthesis. This is one of the highlights of growing outdoor hydroponic plants— however, some unique challenges exist

Grow Season

One of the biggest downsides to hydroponics outdoors is the limited growing season. If you are living in a temperate climate, you will get frost about five or six or seven months a year. That means getting plants inside the building in a greenhouse or stopping to grow. Some plant types thrive at cooler temperatures, such as certain kinds of greens and green vegetables. However, the benefit of a closed interior system that can grow things such as tomatoes and cucumbers year-round is not achieved with outdoor hydroponic.

Pests

In outdoor hydroponics, you'll still have to watch out for aphids, whiteflies, fungus gnats, and all those tiny bugs that can decimate plants. Whether you're growing tomatoes, kale, lettuce, or cabbage, or just about anything else, you've got to look at how pests naturally target plants and fix the issues that could endanger plant health. In comparison, the plants can be naturally secured in a closed hydroponic system.

Plant Media

Most outdoor hydroponic systems have the same irrigation layout as indoor ones-growers are using sterile media plant pots and running water through to nourish plant roots. It means that outdoor growers of hydroponics do not need to worry about weeds. So, no herbicides or hoe rows have to be used. This is one reason for this style of gardening— you get the sun and rain outside, but you cannot get the weeds.

Operational Tips for an Outdoor Hydroponic system

- Solar radiation and sunlight can be very intense; try to avoid long term exposure of the system itself through direct sunlight. A well-developed plant canopy helps prevent direct sunlight overheating of the system.
- You should insulate or cover the hydroponic system with reflective and insulating materials to help protect the roots and the system itself from harm caused by prolonged exposure. UV may be harmful to plastics and rubber when not protected against UV for use in hydroponic systems.

- Make sure that the area where you are setting up your system is level and well-drained. A slope can interfere with how some hydroponic systems are built to work, check your guide or instructions if it is not obvious to you.

- Under good conditions, outdoor plants can grow big in hydroponics, and also very rapidly. Add a float valve or keep an eye on your device or reservoir levels as water can be used quickly compared to indoor production. If water plants are not replaced in order to stay hydrated, fertilizers can begin to build up in the solution, causing nutrient instabilities that can damage production.

Advantages of Outdoor Hydroponics

Build your hydroponic system under the sun. Free sunlight is one of the main advantages of growing outdoors hydroponically. Summer sunlight is far superior to any artificial light source or growing rays. In reality, the sun is essentially the universe's "outdoor hydroponic growing light, so make sure you make the most of it! To build your hydroponic system, choose, if possible, a spot with southern exposure that is properly protected. To decide how the sun moves over your land, you can use a device like SunCalc. You will be surprised by the pace at which your plants grow when all the sun they need is provided.

Keep your water cool. If you grow plants outdoors, they use more water as when grown indoors since it evaporates more easily. That's why you need to ensure that your content stays cool all summer long. There are a few options to do this add cold water to the tank–consider the fact that this will change your pH and EC Put your tank in a sheltered area away from direct sunlight. Load your reservoir slightly to insulate it. Add cold bottles of water to keep it cool on high-heat days.

Purchase a hydroponic water chiller–the most effective but most costly choice. Never leave your reservoir empty as it may be hazardous to the roots of your plants. To prevent this, you should set up a float mechanism, which will activate when low water levels are found, and immediately pour in a fresh nutrient solution.

Lower the EC (Electrical Conductivity)

You may lower the EC of your nutrient solution when it's hot outside because your plants need more water during the season. Reducing the minerals can make it easier to absorb water. You will set your EC to low-to-medium when the plants are in a vegetative growth phase because this growth will be limited by medium-to-high.

As plants bloom and fruit, if you note the leaves' browning to prevent nutrient burning, you may need to reduce the EC.

Enable your plants to cope with hot weather. In the first days of summer, it is a good idea to add some kelp and humic acid to your hydroponic garden nutrient solution. This will lead to an improvement in the plants ' tolerance to excess heat and help them prepare for the hot summer days. The humic acid to the kelp ratio should be 5:2. This combination helps promote root growth and root mass that is necessary to retain more water on hot days.

This blend of extra nutrients also strengthens your plants and helps prevent cell damage from being stressed by excessive heat and too much UV. If you want them to be effective and keep your garden secure and thriving during the summer, remember to take these steps preventively in late spring before the initial stress on the plants happens.

Ensure proper air movement. Besides the free direct sunlight, the natural airflow is another great benefit of an outdoor hydroponics garden. The air movement of this sort helps keep the pores (called stomata) open. It means that adequate levels of carbon dioxide are consumed and that there is the prompt and proper release of the evaporating water and oxygen. A good breeze will also extract some moisture from your plant's leaves and help to keep them fresh during the hottest days. Keep in mind the opposite effect may have too much heat. It will force the plants to close down their stomata to keep the water in. It ensures that you have good air circulation as well as some form of wind protection if you choose the ideal spot for your outdoor hydroponic garden.

Keep Pests Away

Whatever you do, it is possible that you will also have to deal with pests and animals if you want to grow your plants outdoors.

The best advice for minimizing the damage to your hydroponics garden is to grow a few additional plants around it and hope instead they will attack it. You may use specialized detergents or natural pest sprays or insecticide soaps to combat insects and small animals if you do not like the idea of insects and animals that interact with any of your plants.

To make sure that your plants are as healthy and strong as possible, you have to ensure that they are free from pests. Therefore, you should use full-spectrum all-purpose, high-potassium to nitrogen fertilizers. This could cause your plants to weaken because you overdo it with nitrate nitrogen. It would make them more vulnerable to fungi and insect harm. You can also increase the consumption of calcium, which also tends to promote the strengthening of plant cells and also render them more resilient to high or low temperatures. Know that the better the plants are, the more delicious they are, and the greater their vitamins and nutrients. In the outdoor hydroponic garden, you will also be surprised by the bright, healthy colors of plants, flowers, and fruit.

Pros and Cons of Outdoor Hydroponics

Pros

- Scientists all over the world seriously consider the introduction of hydroponics gardening in countries affected by poverty, where the lack of water and nutrients required for the natural development of edible plants. A hydroponic garden also removes the need for clearing and the use of conventional pesticides, herbicides, and insecticides.

- Yes, an outdoor hydroponics garden requires around 10 percent of the water needed by a conventional garden. That means you'll be using ten times less water with such a garden to grow more food.

- An outdoor hydroponic garden benefits enormously from the fact that it can produce food three to four times faster than conventional gardening. This is one of the main points for the hydroponics side in the dispute between soil and hydroponics.

- In urban regions with limited opportunities for conventional agriculture and gardening, such gardening may help develop vegetables or fruit.

- Outdoor hydroponic gardens have another quality that they are adaptable to any region, location, or application. You can horizontally or vertically hang, stack, or set your hydroponic garden to deepen on your preferences and the area you have.

Cons

- The main drawback of building an outdoor hydroponic garden is the considerable initial cost for the equipment. This refers in particular to larger automated systems requiring additional sensors, controls, pumps, and equipment. The less manual work it requires, the greater the automation a garden need.

- The inability to control nature altogether is another disadvantage. Unlike indoor systems where you can completely control the light, temperature, and humidity, this is not quite possible outdoors. Therefore, investment in UV-protected containers and hydroponic components that are able to withstand strong direct sunlight is suggested.

- Extreme temperatures can also inhibit plant growth, which is why your outdoor hydroponics garden needs to be continuously changed, and conditions need to be closely monitored for optimal results.

- Last but not least, you cannot cultivate your plants outdoors under conventional winter conditions, whether in a hydroponic or traditional farming system.

Conclusion

Outdoor hydroponic gardening, as it grows your own organic vegetables and fruit, is not only an excellent hobby for you, this form of cultivation can be the perfect solution to poverty-stricken nations or areas in which people are hungry because of lack of water and farmland. This method of outdoor plant growth is an extremely important staple that can save people from hunger and provide entire communities with self-sufficiency.

By using natural sunlight, you guarantee that your vegetables and fruits grow much faster and tastier without the additional cost of indoor lighting and the regulation of temperature and moisture. With your own specific hydroponic garden, you can also guarantee that your outdoor space, lawn, patio, or other looks so much better. Once you've set up all the components of your outdoor hydroponic garden, you can sit back and enjoy the products of your effort, hard work, and the charm of your own home garden.

4.3 Hydroponic Fruit Gardening

Hydroponics vs. Traditional Gardening

It is best to understand how each planting technique works to decide which system is best for your fruit plants. Soil-grown fruits are raised directly in a soil source, where the plants receive nutrients from them. Hydroponic systems were initially introduced in the late 19th century as a relatively new cultivation method. The plant roots are grown in a hydroponic system in a solution consisting of water and nutrients. Most hydroponic systems also have a substrate to help support the plant roots, such as perlite, sawdust, or clay.

Hydroponic Fruits Gardening

Technically, any fruit can be produced using a hydroponic method, but some varieties thrive in hydroponic conditions better than others. In hydroponic conditions, for example, fruits growing in the wet are like cantaloupe, tomatoes, watermelon, strawberries, blueberries, blackberries, grapes, and raspberries do well. Some picky fruits, such as blueberries, which need very acidic soil conditions, are best grown in hydroponic systems as pH levels, and nutrient content in a hydroponic environment is easier to control. The key to effective indoor berry crops is to know the plant's physiology and natural life cycle, so planting, pollination, and fruiting will all go according to expectation. Although hydroponic strawberries are not an uncommon product and are fairly easy to grow, many berry crops need a little more time and effort expenditure. They're highly rewarding, though. Hydroponic cranberries, blueberries, and raspberries can all be produced with soilless greenhouse cultivation on a limited scale— many in high tunnels to prolong the harvest season and boost fruit quality— but they can also be grown indoors.

Hydroponic Strawberries

Strawberries are the perfect crop to obtain some experience with. The plants are easily available, small, lightweight, and available in a range of different styles of fruiting and cultivars that yield relatively fast fruit. Strawberry types fell roughly into two distinct categories: short-day and day-neutral.

Most of the types of outdoor strawberry are varieties from short days. Hydroponic growers should purchase cooled runners or plugs (called "pre-conditioned" plants), which have been refrigerated for 4 to 8 weeks (34-37° F). And, by covering the clean runners and small plants in moist paper and plastic, growers can chill their own stock and put them in a freezer for four to six weeks.

This way, artificial cooling replicates the cold winter conditions, which are particularly good for those in tropical areas, or where winters are very mild. When planted out into the light and warmth, the plants restart their foliage production cycle of spring growth. They flower fairly fast, followed by fruiting.

Although pre-conditioned runners or plugs are available in some regions almost year-round, this form of planting stock is grown pretty much exclusively for outdoor gardeners and is therefore often only accessible in spring. But indoor growers may need to start raising their own planting stock if they want to harvest seasonal berries.

Strawberry plants are fairly easy to spread from runners; develop at the end of the fruiting season, and there has been a new development of large-fruited varieties that can be ascended from seed. Hydroponic strawberry production systems are versatile. Strawberries can be grown in longitudinal stacks or towers with a good, high-intensity lighting set-up, which allows an amazing display when in fruit. At the lower levels of vertical structures, though, care must be taken, where light and air passage are often reduced, resulting in lower yields and enhanced occurrence of fungal pathogens.

The strawberry plant is highly sensitive to moisture, and the number one cause of strawberry plant mortality is crown/root rot. Beginners are asked to try their first strawberry crop in a free-drying, media-based system such as perlite, or a mixture of 50/50 coconut fiber/perlite combination. Only cubes of Rockwool can function, as long as they are well-drained. This way, it is simple to place the plant with the crown just above the media surface. Drip irrigation systems are favored as ebb and flow will induce salt accumulation around the crown, leading to problems as well.

Strawberries can be well grown on these systems in nutrient film technique (NFT), aeroponic, and different adaptations, but plants must be well protected so that they do not slip down into the nutrient flow just clean plants— that is. Not those originating from the soil— must be used to avoid the emergence of root rot pathogens into the structure. Solution warming is useful at 68°F, especially when starting new plants that have recently received a chilling treatment. The EC rates suggested for hydroponic strawberries differ according to environmental conditions and growing methods. NFT EC levels are estimated to be between 1.4-1.8 cm-1, while media rates from 1.4 to 3.0 are more popular. During the harvest time, a minimum EC of 1.8 is required to maintain good fruit quality from all the systems. Running at moderately high levels of EC and potassium is one way to absorb all sugars (Brix amounts) and aromatic volatiles that add to the distinctive flavor and aroma of strawberry.

Indoor growers can manually pollinate strawberry flowers on a cold setting directed at each individual flower with a small hairdryer, or by gently scrubbing the inside of each open flower with a small brush. Hand pollination must be done soon after the first flowers open every day to ensure a good fruit interface as the pollen only remains useful for two or three days after the flowers open.

How to Grow Hydroponic Blueberries, Cranberries, and Raspberries

In a hydroponic set-up, blueberries, cranberries, and raspberries are less frequently grown than strawberries; nevertheless, they are ideal for soilless growth and benefit from the secure environment of an indoor garden. Cranberries are, of course, a bog plant with long trailing fruit-bearing stems.

For this purpose, they are best grown in an elevated environment, three to four feet above the ground, if the stems will lead downward directly. Dwarf blueberry cultivars are now readily available and can produce high quantities of good quality berries, which have been developed to thrive in containers. Dwarf varieties grow to a height of around two to three feet and can be pruned to manage size.

Dwarf blueberries are the most appropriate crop for those with limited space since raspberry canes need more vertical space to grow and leaf out. The canes of the raspberry expand upright. They are linked in with fruit-bearing stems held in place and pruned to hold the canopy free for air movement and prevention of diseases.

Raspberries are classified into two main types: primo cane (fall or everbearing) and florican (summer bearing). Primo cane types are preferred for hydroponics, as these yield fruits over a long harvest season at the top of first-year canes. They also need less room and resources to grow than forms of floricanes. With strawberry plants, these berry crops are better suited for hydroponic systems based on containerized drip-fed substrate. This is to ensure that the root system does not over-saturate and encourage the potential to move the plants when they need to cool or become too large for available space.

Strawberry crops don't need high heat levels and will thrive under similar conditions as many other fruiting plants. Ideal daytime temperatures are of 72-74°F and night time temperatures of 68-70°F. The light conditions are identical to those of tomatoes and capsicum for optimum fruit production and sugar levels, and plants benefit from a long daytime duration to drive up the daily light integral.

Nutrition is identical for all the berry crops. After initial bud split, a well-balanced vegetative formulation is expected in the early stages, accompanied by a potassium-high bloom or fruiting formulation once the fruit set has occurred. For acid-loving blueberries and cranberries, it is possible to run pH values much lower than other crops, about 5.0-5.5. However, we will continue to grow well in modified crop systems where pH is kept at natural 5.8-5.9 ranges. To grow four styles of berries hydroponically with all three crops, environmental conditions trigger the process of flowering and fruiting. Unlike strawberries, chilling is needed to activate the flowers for a good level of fruiting during the plant dormancy stage. The simplest method of providing chilling for berry crops for smaller indoor gardeners is to transfer the containerized plants outside during winter. Dormancy happens during this period because plants need no nutrients and only limited water. The amount of chilling hours required by berry plants varies somewhat on species and cultivar; however, raspberries and blackberries usually require 200-800 hours below 45° F, and 500-600 hours below 45° F. Any types of low chill" may need 200 hours of chill or less.

There are also several low chill" berry plant varieties established for warmer areas, and these allow 200 or fewer chill hours (these are also suitable for indoor growing). Nurseries also list the number of hours of chill required for each variety they offer.

Once the chilling criterion has been achieved, plants can be moved back to the indoor garden where warmth and light can carry them into productive growth long before outdoor crops begin to stir.

In the indoor garden, however, flowering and fruiting will occur much sooner. Also, berries protected from birds' insects and elements often tend to be bigger, of excellent quality, and high yielding. Another essential element of growing indoor berry is the need for assistance with pollination. These blueberries, cranberry, and raspberry flowers, as with strawberries, need pollination to set fruit.

Greenhouse growers may buy small portable beehives for pollination, but a small indoor garden would need manual pollination. For blueberries, having two specific cultivars and crossing pollinate between these can be an advantage. One of the most satisfying activities in an indoor hydroponic garden is the harvesting of berries. Ideally, berries should be left on the plant before harvesting to ripen and bloom completely. This means the maximum aroma and flavor profile has developed. Perfectly ripe berries are delicate and soft, raspberries require careful handling, and should be eaten after harvest as soon as possible.

Hydroponic indoor berry cropping has become a relatively new trend, rendered more feasible by growing small, lightweight cultivars, and low-chill varieties. Although strawberries may be the easiest to master for new growers, the more demanding blueberries, raspberries, and cranberries should not be underestimated as indoor fruits, if well grown, can be highly productive and have a real sensation of taste.

4.4 Hydroponic Herbs Gardening

It is essential to have a good quality formulated hydroponic nutrient. Most herbs favor low to medium levels of electrical conductivity (1-1.6) and overall dissolvable amounts of salt between 800 and 1200 ppm (measuring overall salts is a way to maintain appropriate levels of nutrients).

A mildly acidic pH between 5.5 and 6.4 is perfect. For a hydroponic herb garden, lighting-5 high-output fluorescent fixtures with 6500 K tubes are perfect options. Run cooler than metal halide lights, which can typically be mounted between 6-12 inches from the plants. They use very little power, and they are cost-effective.

Hydroponic Systems

The hydroponic tower of Foody 8 uses a rising medium such as clay pellets of Hydroton to provide strong anchorage and aeration and is outstanding for herbs. It can be used both indoors and outdoors. Foody 12 vertical garden towers (only for indoor use) use a siphon method that enables water to fall automatically every 2 minutes in each rising pod to pull fresh oxygen to the roots. This function encourages the safe growth of plants and offers a good atmosphere for growing herbs. I have been cultivating hydroponic herbs indoors for over ten years now. Why? Hydroponically grown herbs grow rapidly and have more flavor and fragrance (to my taste) than soil-growing herbs.

Herbs prefer daytime temperatures varying from about 65° F to 70° F, but they can tolerate climbs into the 70s. It's good to replicate weather environments if night temperatures drop at least 10 ° F. Some herbs prefer to be well-drained but don't like continuously damp feet... So, well drainage or oxygen exposure is necessary.

Bear in mind that plants harmed by hot, dry indoor environments are more prone to harm spider mites, whiteflies, or aphids.

Here's a list of the eight herbs that I find grow best with hydroponics:

Cilantro: Cilantro can be used in a number of ways but is especially suited for Asian and Mexican dishes. Cilantro regularly pruning back can help slow the bolting and extend the harvest period. I recommend that new seeds be planted about every 6-8 weeks to maintain successful performance year-round. Cilantro has nutritional advantages.

Chamomile: The two forms of chamomile used most frequently are the German and Roman types. They have been used for their soothing and anti-inflammatory effects since ancient times. Chamomile has nutritional advantages.

Lemon Balm: Lemon Balm is simple to propagate, and the growth is quick. This has historically been used as a natural food flavoring agent, a cosmetic, herbal tea, and widely valued mineral oil. Select leaves, or bunches, for growing. When you have selected them from branches/bunches, tie them in bunches and put them in a cold, dry place.

Marjoram: Marjoram has a gentler, sweet taste, with maybe a touch of balsam than oregano. This is claimed to be "the" meat herb, so all foods except sweets are compliments. This thrives with maximum sun and develops to an 8 to 10-inch compact. On the tips of the marjoram, the plant may form tiny white or pink clusters of flowers. Cut these buds as they grow, to prolong the plant life, and allow further leaf growth — less on the marjoram.

Oregano: Oregano is perfect for pasta, spaghetti and marinara sauces as well as for beef or lamb curries, gravies, salads, soups, and even tomato juice! It can germinate rapidly when propagating in Root Cubes or Fast Rooters. Under high performance T5 fluorescent plant lights in hydroponic systems, it grows extremely well indoors. It is an outstanding plant to complement tomatoes and peppers and is currently growing faster when near basil. The Oregano is an aphid repellent.

Mint: Mint is well adapted for hydroponic production and was one of the first hydroponic plants to be developed. Mint grown in water appears to have wider, more extensive leaves than cultivated mint and is suitable in hydroponic gardens. Using cuttings Mint may be grafted.

Harvesting is easy— just snip the leaves and sprigs as required. Cut the stems about an inch above the rising surface to extract greater amounts.

When grown in a hydroponic device, thyme needs limited fertilization. It propagates well by stem cuttings and is, therefore, the herb without which no cooking should be done! It is an aromatic and enticing plant that requires maximum sun and grows poorly in reduced light. Thyme can be quickly propagated with stem cuttings. However, look out for whitefly and spider mites as sensitive to them as Thymes.

Basil: Basil is among the most flavorful and abundant herbs that can be cultivated and is highly common for hydroponic cultivation. This can be collected and trimmed regularly until it is mature. This needs a pH level of 5.5 to 6.5, and many plants suit well. Compact basil cultivars like "Bush" or "Spicy Globe" make scented and enticing house plants without the need for much room.

Watercress: Watercress is a water-loving herb that can be quickly produced from seed or propagated in a budding plug or growing medium by bits of plant. It's a natural type of herb cut-and-grow which is ideally suited for fresh salads, soups, and watercress sandwiches. The thicker branches are usually cut, so only the delicious leaves are used.

Many other hydroponic herbs that perform well include anise, catnip, chamomile, chervil, chives, coriander, dill, fennel, lavender, parsley, rosemary, and tarragon.

Chapter 5: Assemble a Homemade Hydroponics System

Hydroponic Gardening requires plant growth without the need to use soil. Anyone with a limited amount of space and maybe some time on their hands can quickly create a hydroponic garden. Here's how you do.

What You Really Need:

- A bucket.
- A garden hoses.
- A pump.
- Probably a grow light if you do it indoors.
- A pH test kit. Have buffer solutions as well.
- Clips for plants.
- A nutrient reservoir, ideally 50 gallons.
- PVC Pipe.

Having all this can be pricey, but fortunately, once you have it, you're all set.

Step 1: Location

The first step is to figure out where you would put your garden. Many people are going to put it in a greenhouse, porch, or basement anywhere else in the yard that can suit it up. You can expand your garden in many areas, but an essential step is a reality that you need a position that enables the water & nutrients to fill the field equally. An outdoor garden requires protection from wind and other conditions, and you must be aware of the temperatures. If it is inside a location deficient in light, use some growing lamps. This can help replace artificial light with the sunlight that makes the plants grow.

Step 2: Set Together the Hydroponic

You need to put together the materials. You might need six 6 "PVC pipes with s PVC trellis withstand. You'll need to place a reservoir under the pipe, however. Inside the tank, put a pump to help inject nutrients in the plants. There is also a drainpipe in the tubes, which brings the water back well into the tank. Each tubing will have tiny holes for the nutrients that cover the plant roots. The water jet, too, will carry oxygen by air bubbles. There are a lot of ways one may bring that together.

Step 3: Mix the Nutrients and Water

Fill the tank and then insert nutrients. Check the label and see what you need. It's usually a couple of cups, but it's based on the type of nutrients you might need more or less. Once you've got it all, run the system for an hour. This ensures it's all well combined.

Step 4: Set the Plants into the Growing Tubes

It can be easy to plant the tubes, particularly when you have seedlings. This helps you to bypass the seed hassle, as they can be frustrating to create. Buy good seedlings and get rid of the soil. Place everything in lukewarm water to rinse off. As anything else will damage the plant, make sure it is lukewarm. Gently treat the stems and ensure that there is no soil. It can even lead the nutrients tubes to clog up a little bit. Place them in the planting pot and use clay pebbles or another filler to keep the thing in place. This will enable the plant to remain there without destroying the roots.

Step 5: Time to Tie

When doing that, make sure that you bind your crops to your trellis. This will tie up the plants. Attach it loosely to the top to be the most powerful. Clip and tie the bottoms of a plant. Wind the tips to the plant in a gentle way. Ensure you practice in advance a couple of times.

Phase 6: Turn It On and Have It Reviewed

We must maintain regularly. See the levels of water once or twice a day, every day. Ensure the pH is balanced with the nutrients. Always be aware of the levels of water, and when it is too dry, the pump can fire.

Step 7: Look at the Growth

The plants would grow and cover the trellis after a couple of weeks. Growing in hydroponic environments enables fast growth. Clip and attach and try to ensure the plants are safe. If you don't, you could undo the plants.

Step 7: Look at the Health of Plants

You will try and prove your pest garden. If you see any symptoms of rodents or illness, then you should act accordingly. The other plants can be affected by a plant that is munched or has diseases. Clean out any infected plants and make sure that the pests are handled properly. Pests may include caterpillars as well as other insects. Outdoor growing can have an issue with pests in particular, and if they are indoors, you might want to contact pest control.

A hydroponic system is a task, but you can have a successful crop if you're up to that. At first, getting the system together is a challenge, but if you are up to the task, then you'll have a gardening system that could be even more practical than a standard, soil-based gardening system.

5.1 Making a Simple Wick System

You will see that they are easy to create with very little components after looking at the fundamentals of a Wick system. With that, we'll have to go through the directions for construction. This will use a 3-gallon tank, but as long as you get a second fitting container for your reservoir, you can use any capacity.

Two buckets of the same size are commonly used. One lies inside the other and stands on the side of the first or stands on a stone you placed in your tank of water.

Step by Step

1. Grab a 3-gallon bucket & cut a 3/4-inch hole in the middle of the bottom.

2. Fill your tank with just enough nutrient solution so that it hits just below your grow bucket once it is in the position. For final measures, reserve one jug of the solution.

3. Insert the wick through the gap and guarantee sufficient enough to hit the reservoir's bottom. Outside your bowl, you would have about 1 foot inside your tank and 1 or 2 feet inside the reservoir.

4. Untangle your wick within your growing bowl, then fill up to 2/3rds maximum with the growing medium. (Wicks must be close to the rooting mechanism of the plants, and large enough to be coated with the solution as the levels fall).

5. Place the plant into the bucket or use Hydroton pebbles to fill the top thirds of the pot with a much more growing medium.

6. You should place your growing bucket within your reservoir. It is best to make sure that no light will reach where the nutrients are, as this avoids the growth of the algae.

7. With that of the solution from your bottle, softly cover the water over your plant which keeps the plant roots from sponging moisture from the growing medium.

If you use an air pump as well as air stones, all you have to do is make a tiny hole in the upper edge of your tank and feed into the pipes (change transparent for black tubing), it will provide more oxygen to your solution to help grow the plants.

Maintenance of Wick System

Wick system requires too little maintenance, but sometimes they need some attention. A lot depends on how much maintenance you need to do depend on the size of your wick system. Many of the principles, though, are the same whatever the size of the system. Plant growth may be slower than that of other processes. However, there are a couple of things to support the plants along, including inserting air stones.

These few tips from this manual form of Hydroponic system will help you have the best plant development possible.

1. Using many wicks and plants get sufficient quantities of water as well as nutrients–this depends on the size of your container. For buckets greater than 3 gallons, for example, two wicks can be used.

2. Hold levels of water as high as possible–the nearer the water is to flow, the less distance it requires.

3. Make sure to clean your growing medium after harvest and wash off any salt that builds up. When the water levels decrease, certain rates will rise. Only apply adequate nutrients, and then use plain water to top off.

4. You'll need to use the optical meters to calculate the EC and pH rates.

They may find these sorts of systems are far too simple for some farmers, and they cannot produce the outcomes they want. Although basic in design and execution, these devices are more than suitable for fitting in small areas. As for failing to deliver results, a Wick system is more than suitable for delivering great outcomes for the right plant forms.

This helps farmers to free up some space in a complete system and use it for plants needing less continuous care. On a final note, there's no other hydroponic system that is better suited to new farmers than these. They are the perfect training ground for understanding anything about hydroponics.

5.2 Building a Deep Water Culture System

DWC stands for Deep Water Culture in hydroponics; it's a modification of the standard water culture scheme. As a standard water culture system, a DWC system works just the same, except that the stream is thicker than a standard water culture structure. Although many people call every water culture system a DWC system, water culture systems are not really called "deep water" unless the water is deep at least 10-12 inches.

Water culture systems are among the easiest and least expensive forms of hydroponic systems to be built. Many times, you may create a water culture system from materials that you lay around your home. This concept of hydroponic system is really perfect for comfortably growing plants of small to medium scale. It is not only cheap with very few parts but also very simple and quick to build.

Building a 5 Gallon DWC System

Parts Needed:

- Five-gallon bucket. (you need to make your own lid if needed)
- Aquarium air pump.
- Airline for the pump.
- Bucket for the plant. (You can also use a regular tiny plastic pot)
- Aquarium air stone. (or stones)

- Growing media. (Filling the basket or pot with)

- Black spray paint. (to the light-proof bucket)

- White spray paint. (to reflect light / heat) Plumbing Goop or silicone. (optional)

You can use more than one basket for several plants if your small, growing plants do. Thus, you can set them apart equally. We will expand a medium-sized bucket DWC system plant, plant container, so we will have one larger bowl. You could buy plant baskets that form just about any supply store for hydroponics in several shapes and sizes. They appear like a strainer of spaghetti shaped like a pot of plants. But we used what we might have lying around, instead of purchasing more.

We just used a standard, durable plastic pot that we were washing and cleaning out—a handheld iron soldering. When you don't have either, you can have them for under $10 at any radio shack or even Wal-Mart. If you plant adapted pot for use in the hydroponic DWC method, you could use a drill bit to dig the holes, but burning through the holes gives you a cleaner space, and it's much quicker too. A soldering iron is a good tool to have around if you plan to build furthermore than one hydroponic device.

Once you've gotten the container ready for your herb, you'll have to cut a hole in the 5-gallon bucket cover to fit it in. It's better to cut a test hole into something first, as you will need a new cover (or bigger plant pot) if you get it high. Draw and cut the test hole is a part of the Rotary tool that is used to cut the hole in a DWC framework cardboard lid (box side, etc.) and test the pot within. Use your check hole as the guide and cut it out on your lid if it fits perfectly without dropping through.

Now go ahead and in the 5-gallon bucket lid take out the basket opening. The best way to do that is to use a rotary tool with something like a drill bit and fallowing along the axis (another useful tool for hydroponic systems construction). You could find a rotary machine at the swap meet for about $10. If you have not a rotary tool, you could also use a plastic blade with a jigsaw to cut it out. Only drill a hole that is big enough to accommodate the blades near the line you traced (within the section you cut out). Move the blade inside the hole and slash along the line. You could also break the gap with a soldering iron if you have to. This will take longer and make a lot of dust, but if you need it, it will work.

If your bucket and lid of 5 gallons are already light-proof, you should miss this steep one. But if you put the bucket on your head and see any lights coming through the acrylic, blocking light for DWC system proof isn't light Painted bucket. If not, you should paint it black to avoid light on the outside. Ensure you use a plastic surface spray paint, or it won't stick for long.

You can encourage algae as well as other microorganisms to thrive if you don't stop the sun from getting into the tank. The three elements that increasing algae requires are space, water, and food. The nutrients give the food in the water, so you have to block the light or send it all three.

Bucket coated white to reflect sunlight for DWC system Black materials absorb heat, so keeping the plant's root zone cool is necessary. So now, painting it again, however, this time coating it clean, you'll have a coating that shows light/heat but still prevents light from coming in. Because your color is white over black paint, it doesn't have to be the white paint on plastic surfaces. And it should be a shiny surface so that it won't easily get dirty.

Now to make it much easier for you to lift the lid off to test pH, search Notch at the side of the DWC bucket for the airline's water lever to adjust the nutrients, etc. Cut a small scratch out of the surface of the tank, close to the top to flow through the airline. But far enough down so that Notch passes on the side of the DWC bucket with airlines with a cover connected 1/2 or 1 inch below the cap so that the airline will not be pinched. Thus, you can quickly lift the lid without the need to push or remove the airlines. But you could also use a hack-saw.

Several air stones are going to float. At any hydroponics shop, you might buy certain weighted air stones, but they generally cost much more. We just weigh down the regular Wal-Mart aquarium air blocks. It is quick to do so; it only requires 24 hours to dry. In DWC systems, we used only Aquarium air stone to aerate water superglue several metal washers (to keep them in place) to the base to weigh down the air stones. But as you don't want the metal in your nutrient solution to rust or corrode, we only spray a coat of plumbing goop over metal washers. So, the metal never gets into contact with water. The pluming goop is safe at 100% and will not slip off. You can also use 100% silicone to do so. We just like to use the plumbing goop because, in the long run, it's more durable, and we have always had some at hand.

Expanded DWC hydroponic, the DWC hydroponic program, now you have everything you need to bring together. Attach the airlines to the stone of the soil and position them in the bucket center. Put the air pump in. Put the cap on the lid and attach the basket/pot. Load the bucket with enough good quality water, so the basket/pot bottom is about 3/4 inches under the liquid. Take the lid back off & place a permanent marker on the waterline inside. Build more than one inside, so that you can clearly see it. Even if you have plants growing in them, you will always be able to determine where the water line is connected to the basket/pot.

With the water line indicated and you see how high it's in relation to the plant's basket/pot, the water height can be easily adjusted at any time. So how high would that level of water be? There are many variables, so for all Dwc bucket program with plant basket circumstances, there is no one size fits all solution. There is, however, a thumb rule to go through. That is high enough to make the rising media & rootball damp inside, but not soaking wet. Whether the top inch of the rising media is dry, it is great and even helpful, but should be damp (not dripping wet) 2-3 inches down.

Now blend the nutrient solution in water as per the instructions of the manufacturers. See to it that the nutrients are for plants grown hydroponically. Then check and change the pH if appropriate. When the nutrient solution is combined, fill the basket/pot with growing medium and seedling or plant ready. If you began your own starter cubes seedlings, just fill the bucket with growing medium and place your seeds in it. If you start in potting soil with potted plants, wash away all the soil from roots gently. The easiest method to do this is to fill a pail of water and submerge the roots & soil in it. Then clean the soil gently by hand from the roots when underwater.

When you have the plant in the DWC method, the roots would generally need about a week to start coming out of the Dwc plant bucket hydroponic system with roots basket or container displaying plant. Therefore, you'll like to make sure that your water levels are enough to get plenty of moisture from the root ball. The precise water level will not be so critical once the roots hang down into the nutrient solution.

If your 5-gallon bucket lid is hard to get off at regular intervals, you should cut a hole in it to make things easier and add water to test the pH. And monitor the water level, put a stick in it, or just fill it until you can see water starting to flow out of the airline nozzle.

5.3 Building a Nutrient Film Technique

Nutrient film technique (NFT) is a hydroponic technique in which a shallow watertight stream comprising all the dissolved nutrients needed for plant growth is recirculated in a watertight gully, often known as channels, through the bare roots of plants. The recirculating stream depth should be very small in an ideal system, little more than a water film, hence the term 'nutrient film.' It means that the dense root mat that grows at the base of the channel has a top surface that is in the sun, although it is moist. Despite this, the plants' roots are supplied with a sufficient supply of oxygen.

What is needed to get started:

- (8) 8-ft 2x4's
- (3) Sawhorse Brackets
- (18) Curved metal plant hangers with screws
- Drill and
- 1.5" self-feed bit; you don't want to drill a 2 "hole, or the net cup can fall in. You may be allowed to use the Titanium Drill bit (HGDRBT); however, we cannot promise that a PVC pipe can move through it.
- (8) 3 "PVC pipes 10 feet long
- (10) 3" PVC lengthy sweep elbows
- 3 "PVC shorter sweep elbow
- 3" end cap for PVC pipe
- 1/4 "Black tube (HGTB50-about 6 feet0
- 70 gal Active Aqua Premium White Reservoir with cover (HGRES70K)
- Active Aqua 550GPH Submersible Pump (AAPW550)
- Active Aqua 10"-Pump Bag (AAPB10)

- pack of 2" Net cup (HG2NETCUP)

Methodology:

- Fasten the 2x4's to the brackets of the sawhorse, so you have three parts.

- Dig holes where the legs of the A-frame would be mounted. The 2x4 sets should also be no more than 3.5' apart from each other as the 2x4 on top is only 8 feet long to keep them together. Bury the three pairs of 2x4 sets about one foot deep at such an angle, and they cross in order to make the' A.'

- Put the top 2x4 brackets in between. If you have extra 2x4's, replacing any set of A's with some 2x4 in between would be perfect. Well, you should be operating on a stable picture.

- Screw-in metal plant hangers that give the PVC pipes a steady tilt as they descend to the reservoir (no more than 2% gradient). You don't want the water to spill down the pipes.

- Drill holes, which require the 2 Net cups to fall out without the cup falling through the hole all the way. Using a self-feed drill bit performed right about 1.5 in diameter. Once you cut all your gaps, it is safe to play with a bit of PVC. Place the holes about six apart; on this method, you should also be able to get about 120 holes.

- Hang the PVC pipe on the hangers — split PVC pipes to connect to your key 10-ft pipes at the end of the A-frames. To link PVC, use the lengthy sweep elbows. You could get a suit that's strong enough not to leak out. But if you need to tighten the elbows to the tubing, use some durable PVC adhesive.

- Add the small sweeping elbow to an end pipe that goes into the tank.

- Cut a 1/4 hole and seal the front of the first PVC pipe in the endplate.

- Put one end of the 1/4 tube into the end cap and attach it to the pump the other end. Place the pump inside your pump bag. Assure that the tubing & pump string in the reservoir cover passes through the port.

- Put the PVC and elbow ends over the river outlet so that water goes back into the reservoir. If you want to escape the heat of summer, you should cover the reservoir. In the summer, though, certain herbs do not do as well.

- Fill the tank with water with enough GH FloraGro and FloraMicro to raise the EC to about 1.0-1.5 for greens/herbs; change the pH to about 6.0 if appropriate. Plugin the pump & watch it all run smoothly. I'm even introducing several 5 ml/gal SOS beneficial bacteria to help keep the reservoir clean.

Transplanting:

• This system works well for limited root systems for vegetables and herbs, where the plant doesn't get any larger than a couple of feet. When you try to grow bigger plants (such as tomatoes) or ones with big root systems (such as mint), then the 3 PVC pipes will be clogged.

• In Grodan 1.5 A-Ok Plugs as well as Accelaroot Starter Plugs, you will grow stuff like basil, lettuce, and small herbs directly.

• Or you can purchase tiny transplants in the garden center and wash the soil carefully. Only make sure there's enough of a root ball, so the roots reach the bottom of the PVC as you insert it into the machine.

• Place the transplant in the Net cup and put it into the gap. You should put a 2 Neoprene Insert in the cup to keep the plant (HGNEO2B) if you need to provide the additional transplant support.

Maintenance:

• System runs 24/7; NFT operates like this.

• Change the reservoir nutrients every 2-4 weeks. And in between, keep an eye on pH as well as EC levels.

• Replace any plants that become too mature and possibly clog the network with big root balls.

• **WARNING:** If you are using the whole basil growing device, you'll get enough pesto in your freezer for the next few years!

5.4 Tips and Warnings

Tips to be Successful in Hydroponic Gardening

Thankfully, current trends lead many farmers to switch away from traditional growing methods to hydroponic development because it is more flexible, and the systems can be installed everywhere, from greenhouses to bedrooms. Plants are produced in an increasing medium in hydroponic systems, and a mixture of water, including fertilizer, is distributed, which encourages quality growth.

Procured from two Greek words, "hydro," meaning water, and "ponos," meaning work, hydroponics has come a very long way and is becoming the future of farming. For someone who has no experience in it, it's a daunting growing technique to master, so here are four tips about how to sustain an effective hydroponic growing process.

Ensuring Water Quality

Growers must test the quality of the water supply before it is introduced into a hydroponic system. The pH measures the levels of acid or alkali in the water and is essential to keep track of with pH meter or pH strips. The pH scale ranges between 0.0 and 14.0; 7.0 is neutral, fewer than 7.0 is called acidic, and more than 7.0 is alkaline. In several hydroponic systems, the pH rates farmers like their water to be between 5.5 and 6.5, but where pH values exist, the choice of a grower and the variety of plants getting grown in the system are decided. Multiple nutrients are consumed at different rates, which means that the required pH levels may vary depending on the plant type or the crop's life cycle.

No matter what type of plant has been grown in such a hydroponic system, a grower's water supply requires sufficient EC levels to sustain healthy plants. EC tests the sum of dissolved salts, which are the nutrients or context mineral plants, to stabilize the water. EC correlates directly with the nutrients accessible to crops, so EC testing is essential. The nice news is that farmers will measure their EC rates with EC meters that transfer an AC voltage through them, showing the water's conduct when inserted.

Under any hydroponic system, the water temperature should be between 68 & 72°F. Growers will with a water heater & water chiller hold their water temperatures. This ensures the water is not too warm or too cold to be distributed to the plants.

Will Kacheris, who builds customized hydroponic systems for Grow Span Greenhouse Structures as well as Hydro Cycle Growing Systems, adds, "Using aeration and a UV sterilizer can help growers with unfeasible water to chill out.

It keeps disease down and higher levels of dissolved oxygen so that the plants can grow faster. Aeration of the root region with a bubbling system, such as air stones, also helps to keep the roots clean so that they can consume nutrients freely."

Introduce A Fertigation System

In hydroponic production, the correct application of fertilizer into the water supply is important, since the plants are produced without soil, depending on the right quantity of water and nutrients to thrive.

Kacheris further stresses why precise fertilizer distribution is so essential in hydroponic growing, "The soil generally provides a barrier for salts, acids and bases decided to add to the system, without this natural buffer, growers must be careful not to shock the plants with such an overdose of a chemical." Applying the appropriate amount of fertilizer can be difficult because when the nutrients are mixed inside the system. Without a fertigation system, this can be timely because it implies the grower will have to pour, mix, and test manually, using an experimentation process until the pH levels are right.

The implementation of a fertigation system will increase the efficiency of the process. Kacheris states, "The plants are healthier and are fed regularly, contributing to optimum growth." This won't prevent needing to check the pH levels. However, this does allow it such that the correct quantity of fertilizer is applied every time more precisely, making the cycle smoother. Growers will calibrate their machine at least once a month, preferably once every two weeks, to ensure the right quantity of fertilizer is being added and to make sure pH levels are where they need to be.

"Rising labor costs in the agricultural industry have also been a huge reason for farmers to optimize the fertigation system," Kacheris says. "Comparing to a salaried employee, the system can compensate for itself in a few months which can continue for years and years."

Choose the Best Growth Medium

The absence of soil in a hydroponic method ensures there must be enough so the plants will be propagated in and sustained by allowing the nutrient solution to pass successfully through. The aim of a good growing media is one which requires a reasonable combination of oxygen as well as moisture to be consumed by the roots of the plants.

The mixture of clay pebbles and coco coir is also used in hydroponic processes because the mix preserves oxygen or moisture at an elite level. Clay pebbles are the clay pellets that are inexpensive and popular for keeping oxygen at a higher level, and coco coir is produced from coconut husks that could also easily stand alone as a strong medium in both regions but is costly. Therefore, combining it with grow rocks is sometimes done to keep down prices.

Rockwool is another product that is often used because it's like coco coir. It is excellent at maintaining both oxygen & moisture and is processed in cubes enabling plants to be conveniently put in line. The downside is that it should be tossed out after just one usage.

Clean the System Regularly

Finally, all the above tips could be done perfectly, but when the system is filthy and contaminated, it won't matter. Cleaning a hydroponic device periodically is a vital part of maintaining a major operation because it maintains a plant clean of pests and diseases.

Upon thoroughly sterilizing the whole grow room, growers will clean the nutrient solution tank. It is accomplished by emptying the tank, filling it back up halfway, and using a delusional bleach solution for such an effective wash, ensuring there's no solid content buildup in the piping. Reservoir cleaning is typically done every two or three weeks, but cleaning duration depends on how active operation is. Clogging could also be prevented by having to open the valves for few seconds once a week.

Cleaning down the baskets or grow trays is also crucial in the purification process to prevent pathogen buildup. This process is easy and can be achieved through the use of a scrubby and a 10% bleach solution. A grower could apply the bleach and scrub until they become spotless and afterward wash them out to make the final process. This is generally done with each planting season and after every harvest.

Here are a few useful tips for any grower to run a productive hydroponic growing system. Keep a healthy growing environment and maintain it, ensure good water quality, introduce a fertigation program, and choose an appropriate growing medium, clean the system daily, and you'll consider your project set up for success.

Conclusion

Hydroponic gardening provides one of the easiest ways to grow fresh vegetables throughout the year. It is also a decent alternative for developing in smaller spaces a variety of plants, even indoors. Hydroponic gardening is merely a mean of soilless plant growth. If plants are raised hydroponically, their roots do not feel compelled to search for the nutrients necessary to survive. Instead, they are provided directly with all the nutrients required for powerful, vigorous growth Root systems are therefore smaller, but plant growth is robust. If that is your choice, your hydroponic garden could grow outside. By encouraging plants to grow outdoors, you'll be using sunshine to support the growth of your plants. This is a perfect, economical option for your hydroponic system because you will not have to incur the lighting-related costs. There are certain downsides to growing outdoors, though –the crop is exposed to all the hazards that a typical crop faces: severe weather, unpredictable temperatures, invasions of bugs, and pests. Obscene rain can also be a major problem; it can dilute the nutrient solution and bring the plants at risk of depletion.

Hydroponics systems are used in thousands of variants. If a hydroponic system to grow plants is being built or used. At first, the way hydroponic systems operate may seem complex, but once you know it, you can see how they work, and it becomes easy. Six different types of hydroponic systems are present. All hydroponic systems rely on the six different types, whether they are a type or two or more of the six. In any of the six systems, there are various ways of changing and alter any component. So, once you have heard about how every hydroponic method requires three roots (water, nutrients, and oxygen), you will be able to identify the system type in which you are using hydroponics.

Any fruit can be produced using a hydroponic method, but some varieties thrive in hydroponic conditions better than others. In hydroponic conditions, for example, fruits growing in the wet — like cantaloupe, tomatoes, watermelon, strawberries, blueberries, blackberries, grapes, and raspberries — often do well. Some picky fruits, such as blueberries, which need very acidic soil conditions, are best grown in hydroponic systems as pH levels, and nutrient content in a hydroponic environment is easier to control. Herbs prefer daytime temperatures varying from about 65°F to 70°F, but they can tolerate climbs into the 70s. It is good to replicate weather environments if night temperatures drop at least 10°F. Some herbs prefer to be well-drained but don't like continuously damp feet. So, well drainage or oxygen exposure is necessary.

Bear in mind that plants harmed by hot, dry indoor environments are more prone to harm spider mites, whiteflies, or aphids.

It is easy to build your own simple hydroponic system by using a reservoir of plastic storage, an air pump to aerate the solution of the nutrient or an immersible pump for the liquid to circulate, and growing media or net bottles for plant support. In order to hold the plants and convey water from one end to the other, space-saving structures can be built for those trained in working on PVC pipes. The easiest thing for the beginner (although it may be more costly) is to buy a kit or a ready-to-use setup if you are not that handy. If you do not grow in a greenhouse, you need additional lights to get 12-14 hours of light a day for good growth. This may be a basic LED grow light, which functions for lettuces, greens, and herbs, or high-intensity discharge lamps (HID) for flowering and fruiting plants, depending on what you grow. Start small with easy-to-grow crops like lettuce or basil and work your way too difficult crops as you build trust. Hydroponic growing can be a viable alternative to traditional farming, once you get your feet wet.

Author's Note:

Dear reader, I am pleased that your reading has come this far. I hope my experience and advice on Hydroponic systems can help you start or improve this type of gardening. Your opinions are very important for me. I would love to know your opinions on the book. If you want to write a review, I promise you that I will read it personally.

This is the direct link to the book review: |
http://www.amazon.com/review/create-review?&asin=B085ML9BC7I would not mind if you want to write to me personally, you can do it; as a present, I will send you the free eBook *Organic Gardening.*

This is my email: alfred.mcjames@gmail.com

References

The history of hydroponics. (n.d.). Retrieved from EZ GRO GARDEN: **https://ezgrogarden.com/history-of-hydroponics-2/the-history-of-hydroponics/**

Components of hydroponics and their role. (n.d.). Retrieved from ShopGrowLife: **https://shopgrowlife.com/components-hydroponics-roles/**

Why use hydroponics. (n.d.). Retrieved from EZ GRO GARDEN: **https://ezgrogarden.com/hydroponics/why-use-hydroponics/**

Printed in Great Britain
by Amazon

60642393R00068